Raw Dog Food:
Make It Easy For You and Your Dog

by Carina Beth Macdonald

Dogwise Publishing
Wenatchee, Washington U.S.A.
www.dogwisepublishing.com

Raw Dog Food:
Make It Easy for You and Your Dog
Carina Beth MacDonald

Published by Dogwise Publishing
A Division of Direct Book Service, Inc.
403 South Mission Street
Wenatchee, Washington USA 98801
509-663-9115 / 1-800-776-2665
www.dogwisepublishing.com
email: info@dogwisepublishing.com

Indexing: Elaine Melnick "The Index Lady"
Graphic Design: Anderson O'Bryan, Wenatchee, WA
© 2004, Carina Beth MacDonald

Cataloging-in-Publication Data is available upon request from the Library of Congress.

ISBN 1-929242-09-3   **33614080751125**

Printed in U.S.A.

Dedication

To dogs everywhere, and the people who serve them meals.

Acknowledgments

Too many people to name gave me advice and encouragement — you know who you are and THANK YOU!

Publisher's Note

When Dogwise Publishing set out to publish a book on the raw dog food diet we knew we wanted a book that focused on how-to-feed rather than the science of canine nutrition. We wanted a book that de-mystified the topic and made it accessible and do-able for the busy dog owner. To that end we chose an enthusiastic raw-feeding layperson with a humorous and earthy writing style, Carina MacDonald, to take you by the hand and be your mentor.

Along the way we learned that the topic of whether to feed your dog a home-made, raw food diet incited the passions of both its proponents and opponents. We found that no matter what our author had to say, there was always another way of doing it "right." Therefore we offer you this book as one "right" way to feed raw. We remind the reader that the purpose of the book is to educate and entertain and that neither the author nor the publisher shall have liability or responsibility to any person or entity with respect to any loss or damage caused, or alleged to have been caused, directly or indirectly, by the information contained in this book.

Our author has been cooperative, patient and diligent in her work on this project and a delight to work with. We hope you enjoy and benefit from her efforts. Read on!

Charlene Woodward, Dogwise Publishing

Photographs courtesy of:

Table of Contents

We were just people who were simply trying to improve the life and longevity of our dogs.

CHAPTER 1

Why I Started Feeding Raw Dog Food

This is the tale of how a raw dog food neophyte — Me — began to feed Phoebe, my senior citizen German Shepherd mix, Dutch and Daphne, the rescue Rotties, several fosters and Cooper, my Rottweiler pup RAW chicken bones along with other RAW food and they LIVED! Better yet, they THRIVED! I had always fed my dogs a "better" kibble, select table scraps as well as raw marrow and rib bones to clean their teeth. For years I felt quite smug about what a good and devoted dog-mommy I was. Little did I know that there was a better way.

Dog People Love to Talk

Then, a few years ago, as I was planning to get a new Rottweiler puppy, I began to hear about breeders who instead of feeding dogs a commercial dog food were using a diet based almost exclusively on raw meaty bones and other fresh foods. Hmmm! After kibitzing with about every serious breeder in the Rocky Mountain West, I had not only located my future bundle of fluffy joy, but had learned a new concept …BARF! Bones And Raw Food or Biologically Appropriate Raw Food … raw food diets for dogs that consist of Raw Meaty Bones (RMBs), muscle and organ meat, pulverized vegetables and fruits and miscellaneous scraps instead of commercial food. The BARF diet has been championed by Australian veterinarian Ian Billinghurst in, *Give Your Dog A Bone, Grow Your Pup With Bones* and *The BARF Diet*, Kymythy Schultze in *Natural Nutrition for Cats and Dogs: The Ultimate Diet,* Tom Lonsdale in *Raw Meaty Bones* among others. It made sense!

A Coyote with a Brain the Size of a Kumquat...

I reasoned that if a coyote with a brain the size of a kumquat can figure out how to feed himself without running extensive lab tests, conducting longitudinal studies on other coyotes, or analyzing the molecular structure of oats, it shouldn't be difficult for me to figure it out! Yet I found myself, like many others, intimidated by all the information available, much of it excellent yet often confusing or contradictory. But I continued to read, research and reason.

We always hear that the best diet for *people* is one based on fresh foods with lots of raw fruits and veggies with minimal preservatives. Yet here we are giving our dogs highly processed food, day in and day out. Or in my case, premium kibble supplemented with select table scraps and raw marrow bones for chewing. Now I was being presented with the information to take the logical next step — actually feeding dogs a total diet of real fresh food. It made so much sense! Why didn't it occur to me years ago?

Skeptic that I am about fads and "sure fire" solutions to life's many challenges, I did my own research on the topic. In person and on the internet I met successful dog breeders and owners who told me again and again that a natural, raw, grain-free diet would yield benefits from the elimination of skin problems to curing cancer to little odorless poops. These were not Earth Shoe™ wearing weirdos who sipped spirulina for breakfast. These were serious dog people, who taught obedience and agility classes, raised champion conformation and working dogs and deeply cared for their furry companions. While I wasn't buying into all the "amazing" testimonials, I was becoming convinced that this might indeed be the best diet for my dogs.

Someone to Watch Over Me

A very kind and patient Rottweiler breeder mentored me as I started to feed raw — first to my adult dogs, then to the new puppy Cooper when he came home. She was someone I could relate to as one "Dog Person" to another. We were just people who were simply trying to improve the life and longevity of their dogs.

As part of my education I read all the books on raw feeding available at the time. Although approaches and styles differed, the basic theme was the same — "building a prey animal" for your dog to eat (Schultze — see Resources). This means lots of raw meat and bones and some organ meat. It means vegetables and fruits pulverized to simulate the partially digested stomach contents of the prey animal. Other foods — eggs, yogurt, fish, nuts and seeds may also be fed to ensure a wider range of nutrients. Supplements may be added, either for general health maintenance, or to address specific problems.

What the books *didn't* tell me were answers to the day-to-day questions I had. What's with these peculiar poops? Where can I find cheap supplies? Raw fish bones — ARE YOU KIDDING!? How come he won't eat his vegetables? Can I feed shrimp? Is beef heart organ or muscle meat? It was really nice to have a mentor to ask silly, nervous questions, especially when my vet was initially skeptical, and my friends were aghast at what I was feeding my dogs. I also turned to the internet. It can be a wonderful resource, but the open forum nature of the net means you have to check and double check what you read.

> *We were just people who were simply trying to improve the life and longevity of their dogs.*

Why I Wrote This Book

I know what it's like to be terrified at the idea of feeding raw chicken bones and to go through the anxious phase of trying to micromanage my dogs' diets. I was ready to give it up and go back to kibble! I know how confusing the information is in a single "raw food book" let alone when comparing several books on the topic!

I wish there had been a book like this when I started feeding raw!

Like other "raw feeders," I was lectured to by a vet who thought I was an utter kook. Friends and strangers were appalled at my puppy eating raw meat and bananas *together*. I've poked at what looked like tiny bone fragments in dog poop and found it rubbery (whew!) and I've figured out what to do when the chicken backs are in a 40 lb. frozen lump, I have none defrosted, and my dogs are ready to eat. I also know what it is like to finally awaken to the fact that since feeding raw, my dogs are in fabulous health and allow myself to *relax* and enjoy a long life with my dogs!

I wrote this book to help you make the change to feeding raw by digesting (I couldn't resist) what I've learned and presenting it to you along with practical guidelines on how to manage the "manufacturing" and storage process in an efficient and time-saving manner. My approach to feeding raw dog food is "middle of the road." I've compared several raw feeding approaches and put together a system that keeps my dogs in great health without wearing out the "cook." Honestly, I wrote this book because I wish there had been a book like this when *I* started feeding raw!

I Guess I'm a "Dog Geek"

What are my qualifications for writing on the topic? First — I am not a nutritionist or a veterinary professional — but I am a fanatic when it comes to my dogs' health. I read everything I could on the raw food diet, have been active on several of the raw feeding internet groups, learned much from mentors, and have fed raw food to my own dogs and several foster dogs since 1999.

Much of what I had read in my raw foods diet quest made it seem more complicated than it really needs to be! Realize that what I've written comes from my own perspective and experience and that which I have gleaned from others. I cannot address specific health concerns or esoteric questions on the finer points of canine nutrition. I have included an annotated list of references for further reading, and some well-established internet resources at the end of the book if you want to learn more. I encourage you to find your own way, using this system as your starting point and have fun adapting it to meet your needs with your dog as your teammate.

My Dog Pack

Let me introduce you to my pack of dogs — not just because I want you to meet them but I because I am going to use them as real-life examples to illustrate various aspects of feeding a raw food diet.

Phoebe

Phoebe was my guinea pig-dog. She was about twelve when I started feeding her an all-raw diet. She was a rescued stray I've had since 1992. She's a German Shepherd mix, and though she was always a healthy dog, her age was starting to show. I figured that improvements in her health would be the most noticeable. When I started feeding her raw food, she didn't die. She didn't choke. She didn't get diarrhea, pass whole bones in her stool, get sick, or look unhappy about eating raw chicken parts. She really thrived on this diet. The most dramatic change was when a fist-sized fatty, benign tumor on her side disappeared within weeks, as did all her "old lady" warts. For the first time in her life, her breath did not wilt the houseplants. Three months after switching Phoebe to the raw diet, I took her for her annual checkup. My vet, who was used to anesthetizing her annually for teeth cleaning, asked why I had gone elsewhere to have her dental work done. Her teeth were now that white! Her skin and coat also improved, she lost her strong, life-long doggy odor. Now, at 15 years, she is more kissable than ever. Diet is not a cure-all however. Phoebe's arthritis did not get better, and her tail is still bald from poor circulation.

But her inner puppy comes out when she's handed dinner now —
she totters, bright eyed, to eat with her tail and ears up.

Daphne

Daphne is my little rescue Rottweiler. Like most of my other dogs,
she snarfed up the raw food, too! After one taste of raw meat,
Daphne refused to eat the kibble that had been sent home with
her from the shelter. She was emaciated and riddled with worms,
weighing 48 lbs. on her first vet visit. She's now a healthy 70 lbs.

Dutch

Dutch, my newest Rottie rescue, adapted to his new diet in about
a nanosecond, without even a single day of trouble. He came to
me heartworm positive and in poor health from being an ignored,
chained up, back yard dog. He responded well to the heartworm
treatment and the raw food diet, and within two months looked
like a different dog. His coat lost its dull, dandruffy look and now
gleams. His teeth went from tartar spotted and yellow to brilliant
white. He is very well muscled now and just glows. The person
who helped me rescue him could not believe he was the same dog
that we saved.

Cooper

When I brought my eight-week-old Rottweiler named Cooper
home, his very first meal was a raw chicken wing. He crunched it
down like a little cement mixer and asked for more. He ate pork
and beef neck bones, beef heart, lamb, beef ribs, rabbit, and turkey necks with similar relish. He enjoyed his veggie glop so much
he would slurp it from the bowl before attacking his raw meat.
Bananas were a big favorite...then again, his tastes were not that
discriminating; he had to be sternly dissuaded from eating goose
poop and still has to be blocked from raiding the cat box for kitty
bon-bons. When you remind yourself of what dogs will consume
like hairy termites if given half a chance — socks, dirt, tampons,
books, even furniture — you too will became pretty relaxed about
feeding whole chicken parts! Cooper sailed through puppyhood in
great health, packing on bone and muscle like a weightlifter.

CHAPTER 2

A Raw Diet—What Nature Intended

The rationale behind feeding your dog raw food is that dogs have virtually the same DNA as wolves and other wild canids and should therefore eat a similar diet. Dogs are not designed to eat the grains and carbohydrates that make up 40% or more of most commercial dog food; they get their energy primarily from fats and proteins. Like their wild relatives, the domestic dog has teeth and jaws that are designed for tearing and chewing meat. They have powerful digestive enzymes for rapidly dissolving and digesting meat, bones, and predigested vegetable matter—a wolf will eat almost every part of its prey, including the nutrient-rich contents of the stomach and bowel.

Despite centuries of domestication, dogs are essentially the same animal on the inside as their wild cousins. Their nutritional needs are best met by feeding them the fresh, raw diet they have evolved to thrive on. A raw diet provides lots of enzymes and bacteria to promote a healthy immune system and even a pampered house dog has strong enough stomach acids and a shorter digestive system that easily handle the bacteria load of raw meat.

Better Than Wild

I like to think of this as a "better than wild" diet. Our dogs don't live like wild canids. If a powerful digestive tract, healthy immune system and the speed and strength to bring down an elk are inherited traits, then wolves select for it naturally by mating with the strongest, healthiest alpha wolves—those that survived harsh winters, early illness and were free of congenital defects and physical limitations. Our dogs don't do this and we, not nature, "unnaturally" select them. Perhaps a truly "biologically appropriate diet" would entail throwing them live animals every other day and letting them forage for wild greens, berries and…goose poop.

Of course, we're not going to feed Buster like this! A "domesticated" raw diet will provide a range of different fresh meat and foods—a wolf should be so lucky! You will be feeding human grade meat; fresh fruits, vegetables and eggs, and using select supplements to fine tune the diet or deal with health issues.

A raw meat-based diet provides your dog with naturally balanced nutrition. His teeth and gums will be cleaner and healthier from chewing raw meaty bones. The animal fats help his skin and coat become supple and glossy, the proteins provide energy and vitality. The bones and natural cartilage in the diet will grow strong bones and healthy joints. When you remove cooked, processed meats and cooked grains from his diet, doggy odor, yeasty ears and chronic infections are often alleviated. There is even some evidence that common afflictions of our pet dog population like cancers, diabetes, epilepsy, and severe allergies are exacerbated or even caused by feeding commercial dog foods.

A raw meat-based diet provides your dog with naturally balanced nutrition. When you take control of your dog's feeding, you are taking a big step in bettering his overall health and vitality and quite possibly his longevity. He will love meal time more than you ever thought possible and will get a great deal of primal satisfaction and both physical and mental exercise from chowing down on real meat and bones.

Kibble…Poison or Profit?

I think most veterinarians honestly believe that the safest and most nutritionally complete way to feed your dog is by using commercial food. This is what they have been taught for decades in school. Certainly feeding kibble is convenient—toss it in the bowl, occasionally vacuum up grit and chunks and that's about it. It's not like feeding your dog pure arsenic or anything. However,

it is important to realize that pet food manufacturers heavily fund veterinary school animal nutrition classes, and that these companies have done the most research on companion animal nutrition. Large pet food manufacturers may well know what's best for your dog. They just don't put it in a bag of kibble!

Given a choice, which would YOUR dog choose?

Vets may be unwilling to recommend a better home prepared diet for fear that clients will not take the time to learn how to feed their animals properly. It's increasingly common for the family pet to be overweight from overfeeding, and I have met otherwise educated folks who haven't heard that cooked bones can kill a dog, so perhaps the vets are just being realists. On the other hand, given a choice, which would YOUR dog choose?

Grains...Good or Evil?

Dogs are not engineered to gain a significant portion of their nutrition from grains. This explains the large, soft stools excreted by most kibble-fed dogs. It is clearly processed poorly by the dog. Many vets agree that corn, wheat and soy may cause allergies, skin and coat problems. Overfeeding grains may be a big factor in the frequency of canine obesity today. This in turn may cause or aggravate many other health problems.

Grain-based diets promote bad dental health and that can lead to systemic infections and weakening of all major organs. I have seen estimates that 85% of all dogs over the age of three suffer from periodontal disease, largely from feeding a soft mushy kibble diet. One of the first benefits of a raw diet, often noticed within a couple of weeks, is improved breath and whiter teeth. I always gave my dogs plenty of raw chew bones when I was feeding kibble, thinking that was enough. It wasn't. Once I gave my kibble away and went 100% raw, my older dogs' breath became sweeter within days, and their teeth steadily became whiter and cleaner.

Dogs did not evolve to eat grain, yet this is mainly what we have been feeding them for the last sixty years.

Yes, there are decent kibbles on the market. You are probably feeding one now. However, all contain grain in one form or another, and a cornerstone of the raw feeding concept is that grain is wholly unnecessary for dogs. Grains are often used as fillers, and are the "glue" that holds the other ingredients in those little pellets. They provide, at best, an inexpensive, low quality protein source. Most grains are poorly digested, hence the large smelly poops they produce. Dogs did not evolve to eat grain, yet this is mainly what we have been feeding them for the last sixty years or so. Kibble contains cooked, often low quality ingredients that have had most of the nutrients, enzymes, and antioxidants "boiled" right out of them. These nutrients are then often replaced by synthetic supplements. Dogs have absolutely no need for such a high carbohydrate diet. A wolf eats very few carbs. Added to this, most run-of-the-mill kibbles are often so laden with preservatives and salts that the dog has to drink tons of water.

Where there are allergies, yeast infections, GI upsets, poor dental health, obesity, and cancer, grain may be the major culprit.

Questionable Meat

Very little meat that goes into kibble is considered fit for human consumption. Some cheaper kibbles use "4-D" meats—dead, diseased, dying and disabled. Some people reason that this is not so bad; after all, wolves often eat the weakest prey animals, which are often 4-D! However, remember, the wolves eat UNcooked, UNrendered meat. But reports of road kill, euthanized pets from animal shelters, and rancid restaurant grease being rendered into dog crunchies do bother me (Goldstein; Martin). And consider this, you might think that since "Meat meal" is the first ingredient listed, your dog is getting plenty of meat, but if more than one of the next few ingredients is some kind of grain product you're probably going to be feeding your dog mostly grains.

Understanding Dog Food Labels

Here's a quick tutorial on understanding some of the terms in kibble ingredients. Let me tell you it is WAY different from reading a human food label:

Meats. If meat is identified simply by source — lamb, chicken, and beef — this is best. Typically this indicates higher or human grade meat. This is also sometimes listed as "meal" (i.e. beef meal) meaning the meat has been processed and all the water removed. The terms "animal digest" or "animal byproducts" are generally found on cheaper foods. Not identifying the source indicates that they are getting the meat from several sources. "Animal fat" or "tallow" can be fats from animals or it can be restaurant grease, a common ingredient in kibble.

Corn gluten meal is a common herbicide, though it has been deemed by the EPA as "non toxic" to humans.

Grains. Kibbles high in corn or wheat are best avoided. These are particularly cheap grains and are often associated with allergies and yeast infections. This is why hypo-allergenic kibbles typically have rice as the primary grain source. Corn gluten meal and brewers rice have already been used in other food manufacturing processes and therefore their nutritional content has been depleted. For example, brewers rice is a by-product of the beer industry, and corn gluten meal is a by-product of manufacturing corn syrup. It's interesting to note that corn gluten meal is a common herbicide, though it has been deemed by the EPA as "non toxic" to humans…hmmm.

Preservatives and Stabilizers. BHT, BHA, or ethoxyquin are common preservatives. These have been associated with a number of serious health complications and behavioral problems, including some cancers (Goldstein). Ethoxyquin was developed as a rubber stabilizer and is also used as an herbicide. These ingredients are allowed in small amounts in both pet foods and some "people" food. There are many who think that there has been inadequate research on the long term effects of these and other preservatives, and may be contributing to cancers and other chronic illnesses in both pets and people in industrialized nations. In response to public concern, many manufacturers are switching to "mixed tocopherols" which are mixed antioxidant vitamins such as E, as preservatives. Of course it's necessary to use preservatives to prevent fats from becoming rancid, the food from mold, or the meat ingredients from turning rotten, but isn't it better to simply feed FRESH?

So, you still want to feed kibble?

In addition to heavy preservatives in most kibble, there are texturizers, flavor enhancers like salts and sugars, fat stabilizers and artificial colorants. Sure—most of us eat a lot of these things. But in every single meal, during our whole lives? I wouldn't eat a diet of 100% processed foods, and I won't feed it to my dogs either. Don't you think it's odd that we humans are told that fresh wholesome food should form the basis of our own diets—that the less "processed" foods we eat, the better, while what is supposed to be optimum nutrition for our pets is...you guessed it, 100% processed food? Food that has had the living enzymes and many nutrients boiled out of it—to be replaced by synthetic or cooked nutrients. Food that hasn't been "fresh" in months, perhaps years.

CHAPTER 3

Myths, Fears and Anxieties

Myths and fears abound—and I experienced them all. You may be, as I was, horrified at the notion of feeding your dog raw bones and meat. You may think that if your pooch doesn't die from bacterial poisoning, the bones will lead to a gruesome death. Won't they? You have been warned for years never to feed table scraps. After all, the dog food folks have carefully determined just what your dog needs, haven't they? You may be nervous that your dog will miss some vital nutrient and be undernourished. Perhaps you think a home-prepared diet will be too expensive or time consuming. I found it intimidating to read about people who feed over twenty daily herbs and supplements, or those who spent hours weighing and calculating their dogs' daily intake. Fear not!

Bones...The Really Scary Part

Dogs eat non-digestible dirt, rocks, socks, tampons, plastic squeaky toys, and rawhides. They vomit, choke, poop out foreign objects, sometimes need veterinary attention...these are real dogs in real life. One of my Rottweilers had to have three feet of Christmas tinsel pulled out of his butt by a vet. I know a woman who lost her champion German Shepherd because he choked to death on a tennis ball of all things. A neighbor's Cocker ate a sock resulting in an impaction that would have been the end of her without surgery. Every veterinarian you talk to will have stories of weird things ingested by dogs needing medical intervention—my old vet had an x-ray from a Labrador who ate an entire braided rug.

Can dogs die from eating raw bones? Of course—they can die from eating just about all the other things they eat too! There are risks you can avoid completely, risks you can minimize, and risks you can accept as only a theoretical possibility. Just as every activity carries some risk, we are willing to accept risk when we feel it is minimal compared to the benefits. And feeding raw has HUGE benefits. Remember to NEVER feed cooked bones. These are not well digested by dogs and can splinter easily.

Raw Meaty Bones can be placed in two categories; RMBs that are part of a *meal* and are consumed entirely—or almost entirely—and RMBs that are *recreational* that is bones that are chewed on, left, returned to, left and so on. Recreational bones for one dog may be a meal for another. Deciding which RMBs to feed depends on how your dog eats. Daphne, Dutch and Phoebe all chew their food thoroughly—so I feel comfortable giving them any kind of bones, even the large, weight bearing ones. Cooper gulps his down in a nanosecond. I call the chicken wings I feed him "sliders" because they slide right down his gullet in a single crunch. If your dog eats like Cooper you can try encouraging him to slow down by holding one end of the food while he eats, or feeding separately from other dogs so he doesn't feel like he must inhale his food faster than everyone else! I often feed Cooper frozen or partially frozen RMBs because this forces him to chew a bit. Stay within your own comfort level with this. Some people smash the RMBs with a hammer or meat-tenderizing tool first. And don't forget, grinding is always an option. This will eliminate any fears you have!

Remember to NEVER feed cooked bones. These are not well digested by dogs and can splinter easily.

Creepy Crawly Bacteria

How real is the risk of salmonella, e.coli, and related illnesses? It can happen, but remember, dogs are physiologically equipped to deal with a much heavier bacteria load than we are with their short, very acidic, digestive systems. Your dog has probably eaten kitty bonbons, slurped out of the toilet, cleaned his personal areas, and eaten road kill (if you would let him) without getting ill. If your dog is in generally good health, you too can start feeding raw.

I think that animals and humans alike benefit from healthy exposure to bacteria. Everyone in this house is really healthy and my housekeeping skills are somewhat lacking—make that "relaxed." It seems to me that we are designed to live side-by-side with those creepy crawly things. There are bacteria, including salmonella and e-coli, all over your house right now. Crawling on every surface in your kitchen, your bathroom and all over your skin...sorry to sound gross, but it's true!

Most people find that they have fewer infections and illnesses in their raw fed dogs.

Most people find that they have fewer infections and illnesses in their raw fed dogs. I have not had a sick dog since I started this diet (except for the time Cooper, at 10 weeks old, got a sinus infection from getting dirt and bird poop jammed up his nose from rooting in it). If you are considering feeding a dog with a *severely* compromised immune system (i.e. fighting cancer), I suggest you get some supervision from a good, raw-foods knowledgeable veterinarian or postpone feeding raw until the dog has recovered.

Sanitary precautions are common sense and are probably more for human protection than dogs: use good kitchen hygiene. Any time you have to cut up or handle meat, wash counters, hands and utensils thoroughly. Some people use antibacterial sprays or throw-away wipes, others use natural cleaners like grapefruit seed extract. I also suggest using non-porous dog bowls. Stainless steel is perfect. And plastic cutting boards are easily cleaned in the dishwasher.

Doesn't Fido need "complete balanced nutrition" every day?

Realize this is a meaningless advertising catch phrase! It is ridiculous to think that every dog on the planet will get optimum nutrition from a bag of kibble. There is no such thing as a "Complete and Balanced Diet"—for dogs, for people, for cattle—no living organism *must* have every single nutrient in identical proportions for every single meal of their lives. If every dog food on the market was truly "complete and balanced" as the advertising claims, then every food would have to have the same ingredients and composition, wouldn't they? And if XYZ Kibble Corporation comes out with a "New and Improved" formula then what the heck have they been selling us previously? "Old and Inadequate" formulas?

Your dog can and will eat a very healthful, fresh, raw "complete and balanced" diet...and she will thank you everyday for it!

I have met a healthy 23-year-old Schnauzer mix that has never eaten meat in his life, only a cooked vegetarian diet. A friend's 20-year-old mutt Chester has eaten nothing but the cheapest kibble his entire life. He has horrible teeth and he smells, but he is old and loved. The point of this diet is balance over time—most nutrients are stored and utilized as needed in your dog's body, just as in our own bodies.

In short: Your dog may live a long life on kibble. Many do. But why not seek an optimally healthy life? Dogs are designed to eat raw meat. They have big sharp teeth and strong jaws for tearing and chewing meat. They have short, acidic digestive systems for quickly processing raw meat and bones. These simply are not animals designed to eat a grain-based, processed diet. Your dog can and will eat a very healthful, fresh, raw "complete and balanced" diet that you will lovingly provide—and she will thank you every day for it!

But what if my vet says "no people food"?

Oh, as if dogs are animals designed to thrive on a diet comprised only of bizarre, little, processed-to-death pellets and will be harmed somehow by actual food. Now that is a weird notion isn't it? One of the ways dogs adapted to coexisting with humans was by being natural trash-eaters. Early dogs learned that living around people provided them with easy pickings. If begging is an issue, that is a training concern, not a dietary one. Mine are trained not to beg and they are never fed at the table. They lie quietly and politely drooling, because they know they'll get to lick the plates clean when we're done.

No doubt most vets feed their own dogs commercial food. Plus, they've probably become so used to de-impacting anal glands, treating yeast infections and cleaning teeth, they think this is normal! If your veterinarian is less than enthusiastic about this diet for your dog, you have several options. If you like your vet and have a good working relationship with her on all other matters you could say nothing. After all, if you feed kibble, you wouldn't necessarily tell your vet which brand, would you? If your dog is healthy and only goes in for routine care, there really isn't a need to share diet tips! If you do decide to discuss this diet option and your vet seems interested, offer to lend her books or articles that might be educational, or offer up your healthy dog as proof that feeding raw bones isn't lethal.

If begging is an issue, that is a training concern, not a dietary one.

If your vet absolutely refuses to bend in any way, the philosophical differences in dog care may be too great to bridge. If you cannot agree to disagree, it may be time to look for a new vet. Call around or check with local raw feeding folks to find out who they use. There are many veterinarians who are quite supportive of "alternative" diets and lots who actively promote it. My current veterinarian will not promote raw feeding, however, he has no problems with my doing so. He knows my dogs and knows they are healthy. In fact, they don't have to visit the vet much, but he is close by and his staff likes my dogs so we drop in occasionally to say hello and get treats!

Don't they need kibble to keep their teeth clean?

Of course not! Dogs don't get cleaner teeth by eating kibble, any more than you will by eating cookies. Those crunchy little nuggets provide almost zero teeth cleaning benefits for big sharp teeth. Ever looked at your dog's mouth about an hour after eating her doggie bits? All that goop is still smooshed between her teeth, fermenting away. One of the most immediate benefits most people see with a raw diet is sweet breath and whiter teeth. Often this difference will be seen within days. One of the most common reasons people bring their pets to a vets' office is for dental concerns. Wouldn't you like to be able to throw away that reminder card from your vet "February is Pet Dental Health Month"?

Will raw bones harm their teeth?

Anything is possible. My old Phoebe has a broken canine tooth, which does not bother her at all. Who knows how it broke? Certainly, if you feed nothing but kibble, and your dog never chews on anything hard, you will avoid ever having a chipped tooth — maybe. Of course by feeding kibble you may get decaying, yellow teeth and poor gum health too which can cause heart problems, suppress immune response and compromise kidney functioning. Take your pick!

If they eat it up, it's nutrition.

If they gnaw on it for hours, that's recreation.

I am absolutely amazed by the bones my dogs can eat and pass out the other end in small, crumbly droppings. I feed them beef ribs as recreational bones rather than beef leg or knuckle bones. Large, weight bearing bones such as these are inherently harder and it's possible over time that they might chip a tooth. You can safely feed rib bones to large dogs or beef neck bones to smaller dogs for recreational chewing purposes. Smaller bones like beef necks might be a quick meal for a large dog, but it would be a recreational bone for a small dog. Your dog will let you know which is which! Rule of thumb: if they eat it up, it's nutrition. If they gnaw on it for hours without really ingesting it, that's recreation.

You should do periodic checks of your dog's teeth and watch out for signs of discomfort or sudden unwillingness to chew. Look for signs of uneven or excessive wear. Some dogs have thinner or softer enamel and it may be smart to give them more ground RMBs or softer RMBs rather than big beef femur bones. I have given my dogs large raw bones to chew on for many years and no dog in my care has ever had dental problems as a result. Now, by combining the sheer cleaning power of gnawing on bones with the benefits of a raw food diet, they have even better dental health as well as overall health and no cleaning bills too!

Isn't this diet really expensive?

There are astonishingly wide regional differences in prices, and much depends upon how resourceful you want to be, as well as availability where you live. You do not HAVE to feed organic emu or rabbits. You can buy all the ingredients for the raw food diet at your local grocery store and you can cut your costs even further by watching for sales. If you stick to a wide variety of inexpensive meats, raw meaty bones and beef heart your dog won't be missing anything nutrition-wise and your expenses will be equal to or less than "better" kibbles on the market.

A rough comparison of kibble vs raw dog food might look like this: A 40 lb. bag of premium kibble costs on average about $40 a bag. At my current feeding rate, I figure my dogs would go through 2½ to 3 bags a month. **Total: $100.**

An average month of feeding raw dog food at 6 lbs. per day to feed 360 lbs. (combined) of dog might include:

80 lbs. of chicken backs = $30.00

20 lbs. whole rabbit = $25.00

50 lbs. other meats (beef heart, ribs, necks, fish, pork or turkey necks, ground chuck etc.) at .69/lb. = $20.00

4 dozen eggs, 2 quarts of yogurt, a few veggies = $10.00

Total: $85.00

This is a rough estimate. Some months are less if I get an especially good deal as when my local wholesaler gives me cases of chicken gizzards, or I get venison from my neighbors. Some months are more if I get extra rabbit, or forget to order enough bulk RMBs and have to buy more from the grocery store.

Feeding raw food can be a lot cheaper than premium kibble, especially if you factor in savings on vet care for things like dental work, allergies, parasite control, anal gland issues, etc. My dogs make very infrequent visits to the vet, mainly for annual heartworm checks and vaccinations.

Isn't this diet really time consuming?

The time spent in preparation is minimal, especially once you get into the groove. Factoring in one or two monthly trips to buy meat (usually combined with other errands) and the little time I spend making up the veggie glop and dividing the meat into separate bags, I'd say it takes perhaps one to two hours a month. Maybe my VitaMix™ blender, affectionately referred to as "The Cement Mixer", spoils me. It is very powerful and quickly reduces vegetables into thick glop for the dogs. Even pre-VitaMix, using a food processor, I spent less than three hours a month obtaining and preparing their food.

Isn't this diet messy to feed?

My dogs eat their meals outside or in the garage. They are short-haired breeds not to mention "enthusiastic" feeders who consume their meat in mid-air. The glop and anything fed in a bowl

gets swiftly hoovered up and then bowls are licked to a spit-shined finish. Some people designate an area of the kitchen or laundry room floor as the doggie dining room while many others feed in the crate with the sleeping blanket removed. You can also lay down newspaper, which can be thrown away, recycled, or used for garden mulch! Or old sheets, vinyl tablecloths —anything that can be easily cleaned. Many raw feeders, like the owner of this Leonberger, allow their dogs to dine on the patio. And yes, that is a whole chicken she's eating. They are BIG DOGS after all!

For long haired dogs, or those with beards and mustaches, the trick is to clean them quickly after they eat and before anything has a chance to dry. Dry shampoo works well for spot cleaning and is considered safe. Or use a warm damp rag with a pet-safe cleaner on it. Those stretchy cloth snoods sold

> *If your dog had a taste for killing chickens before eating raw, that won't change!*

by pet suppliers for keeping long-eared show dogs' hair-dos are also handy for keeping your dog's ears out of the way. Here's a neat trick, if your fluffy dog will cooperate: drop something like a tennis ball or water resistant treat into a big bowl of water. As Fluffy dunks for it, she'll get her face all wet and you can just towel her off!

Will raw meat make my dog bloodthirsty?

Nope. Mind you, if your dog had a taste for killing chickens before eating them raw, that won't change! Some people have noticed an increase in food guarding in their multi-dog households. Feeding the dogs in separate locations or in their crates easily solves this. If eating raw meat made dogs vicious, how likely is it that they evolved as protectors, herding dogs, and all around working companions? For hundreds and hundreds of years, dogs have hunted and eaten raw meat while bonding to their humans. It's a stretch that dogs make a connection between a raw chicken back that comes out of the refrigerator and an actual chicken. Dogs think much too concretely for that.

My 100% raw raised Cooper has been to a couple of herding trials. He was a lousy herding prospect. He just wanted to make friends with the sheep and was more interested in eating sheep poops than herding anything. He doesn't have much of a prey drive. When we encounter ducks and pheasants on walks, he will give half-hearted chase and then turn back. So much for going after poultry he has to catch himself! Human-provided raw meat and bones are another matter. After all, he probably reasons, the meat comes de-furred and de-feathered, in handy dandy pre-cut portions and you don't have to chase 'em.

I've Read About Breed Specific Diets...

I have read of breed specific diets based on the origin of the breed too. I really think this is micromanaging doggie diets a tad too much. The basic structure of a dog is the same, whether a Basenji or a Poodle. Certainly, some dogs, regardless of breed, may have some food intolerances (or preferences!). This is the beauty of a raw diet. It can be tailored for the dog's needs. If you want to feed your Poodle duck a l'orange and truffles, your Husky seal meat and herring, or egg rolls to your Shar Pei, go for it. I think it's unnecessary and a bit silly, though. I evolved from Scottish stock, and I assure you, I'm quite healthy without ever eating haggis.

CHAPTER 4

Raw Materials

So — what *will* you be feeding your dog?

Here's a basic list of ingredients...

Raw Meaty Bones

Muscle (boneless) meat and fish

Organs — liver, kidney, heart, etc.

Vegetables, fruits

Eggs

Other optional foods: yogurt or other dairy, apple cider
vinegar, molasses, grains, leftovers

Supplements

My recommended proportions are roughly as follows:

50% RMBs

20% muscle meat

5-10% organ meat

20-25% veggie glop, eggs and "other"

Meat...the heart of the matter

The main component of the raw dog food diet is meat. It is fed in
three ways: Raw Meaty Bones, boneless muscle meat and organ

meat. "Raw feeders" in the U.S. use lots of chicken because it's inexpensive, widely available, and well tolerated by most dogs. But don't think of this as the "raw chicken diet" because you should be feeding a variety of raw meat with bone. Pork and beef necks are big favorites around here and because I have a lot of fun searching out new and different foods, I've included a wide range of meats

to feed. Shown here are rabbit, beef ribs, lamb, and chicken parts.

Dogs get their energy primarily from fats and protein and RMBs provide amino acids, enzymes, protein, fat, minerals and nutrients in abundance. Feeding too much muscle meat without bone can easily create a calcium deficiency; hence boneless muscle meat is a smaller part of the raw dog food plan. Too much bone at one meal can cause constipation, hence we feed meatier bones in a meal. Depending on which raw food guru you follow, the RMB amount will vary from 50% to 70% of the total diet. Feeding small amounts of organ meat, especially liver, equal to 5-10% of the total diet, is important because vitamin A and several other vitamins, minerals and Omega-3 and Omega-6 essential fatty acids (EFAs) are very concentrated therein. At least one raw feeding expert (Schultze) says that if you feed lots of backs you don't need to bother with organ meats because they have little shreds of organ meat attached already.

Too much bone at one meal can cause constipation, hence we feed meatier bones in a meal.

Cluck Cluck. The bulk of what I feed my dogs are chicken backs. They are inexpensive, have great meat-to-bone ratio, plenty of fat, are high in essential fatty acids (EFA's) and usually have little pieces of organ meat attached. Most commercial chickens are killed young therefore the bones are soft and therefore easily digested. There is a lot of variability in size though, especially with backs. Sometimes the ones I buy weigh just a few ounces and are very meaty, other batches may weigh as much as a pound and are much fattier. Chicken wings and necks are also a very good basic RMB. When whole fryers are on sale, I stock up. Much of the meat goes for human consumption and the dogs get the rest. Cornish game hens make a wonderful meal too, and chicken gizzards are inexpensive and much appreciated around here.

When whole fryers are on sale, I stock up. Much of the meat goes for human consumption and the dogs gets the rest.

Gobble Gobble. Because turkey necks are low in fat and inexpensive, I often feed them to my geriatric Phoebe, who needs to watch her waistline. Some people grind these, others chop them into very small chunks, and some leave them whole so their dogs are forced to chew them slowly. It depends on the size of your dog, really. I also use ground turkey sometimes, and turkey backs if I can find them. One word of caution about larger turkey bones like wings and legs — many people, myself included, do not like to feed these because the bones seem harder and more brittle than other poultry bones.

Moooo. Beef necks are inexpensive and have plenty of meat — they're great RMBs for many dogs. Ribs are pricier, but I purchase them by the case to keep the cost down. The dogs spend some time chewing the meat off, and then the ribs are good for hours and hours of gnawing. I've found beef heart very inexpensively, too. While heart is technically an organ, most of the tissue is muscle so I feed it as muscle meat. My dogs get cheap ground beef a few times per month, and occasionally I'll find whole chuck roast on sale, which can make it cheaper than ground beef. I sometimes buy soup leg bones for the dogs to chew on, but take them away after a couple of days. Once they get dried out and hard, they can be tough on a dog's teeth.

Baa, Sooooo-ey. I believe in feeding a wide variety, so I sometimes feed lamb shanks and pork necks or steaks. However, these are fairly rich meats and can be expensive, so they're an occasional indulgence! Trichinosis is rare nowadays since federal legislation in the mid-1990s prohibited the feeding of raw meat garbage to pigs. The Centers for Disease Control suggests freezing pork at 5° F for 20 days to kill the trichinella parasites if you want to be completely certain the meat is safe. Make sure your freezer is actually cold enough. Sometimes pork roast or pork steaks go on sale and I stock up.

Fishies. If feeding locally caught fish, do some research about the safety of feeding raw (or even cooked) fish to your dogs. Check with your local fish and game department. Many parasites, but not all, can be killed by freezing for at least a week. Warning here: Pacific salmon contains life-threatening bacteria. To be extra safe, consider avoiding all raw salmon. Some people poach boneless fish, whether store bought or wild caught. Phoebe loves raw fish, and would give up her doggie soul for shrimp. The Rottweilers think fish is for playing with, not eating. Daphne masticates hers into fish slush (preferably on the carpet) and rolls on it. Cooper prefers to bury his. However, they all love canned mackerel (or salmon, if they've been Very Good Dogs). I keep cans on hand for when I forget to thaw enough meat or just for variety. Canned fish is cooked but still nutritious. They'll also eat raw smelt as long as I feed them frozen. Go figure. Many people feed whole raw fish regularly and the bones are digested just as well as any other bones. If the idea of feeding a large bony fish makes you nervous or if your dog just won't eat one, try the smaller fish like smelt or anchovies. If you have a dog that absolutely refuses fish, be sure to give her fish oil supplements for Omega 3's.

Many people feed whole raw fish regularly and the bones are digested just as well as any other bones.

Other Weird Meats. I've found free, or cheap venison, elk, rabbit, emu by checking internet supplier lists, calling local butchers who dress out game, and letting hunter-neighbors know I'll take carcasses off their hands. There has been a recent proliferation of rabbit purveyors selling rabbit for dogs — check the internet for suppliers in the Resources section. It may not be the most inexpensive meat but I have started feeding it 2-3 times per week.

Rabbit tends to be fairly lean, and many suppliers have organically raised rabbit meat that can be ordered whole or ground — bones, guts and all. If you have to have it shipped, be aware it can be cheaper in the wintertime when lower temperatures mean more time can be allowed for shipping, otherwise you might pay a premium for overnight or two day shipping.

The first time I fed rabbit to my dogs, Phoebe ate it but she'll eat almost anything that has eyes. Cooper refused to touch it at all. Dutch took one sniff, wrinkled his whole face up and backed away at high speed as if I'd offered him plutonium. And sweet Daphne scattered the bits all over the garage floor and rolled on them. It took a few more tries, now they all love their bunnies! Sometimes you just have to offer your dog something more than once for them to try it.

Some people with toy breed dogs order snake food including chicks, rats and mice.

Some people with toy breed dogs order snake food including chicks, rats and mice. Apparently these can be ordered skinned or whole, packed in styrofoam trays like cute little chicken drumsticks. I have included some established suppliers in the Resources section at the end of the book. Goat meat? Why not! If you are very adventurous (and don't mind your vehicle getting messy) try finding a processing plant that will let you have trim or left overs. I have even brought home entire cow heads in winter. I know. It's quite macabre, but the dogs really adore them. If you have large dogs, ask a wholesaler about ordering whole beef necks. They are very large, and provide several days of happy gnawing.

Organ Meats. My dogs get organ meat; usually beef liver, but sometimes kidney. They also get small pieces of organs with their chicken or turkey backs, and when I feed whole ground rabbit the innards are included. Organ meats are very rich and best fed in small amounts at a time. In fact, giving some liver to a constipated dog is one way to get everything moving, so to speak. Since my dogs get a little chicken guts most days with their chicken backs and ground rabbit, therefore I only feed organ meat a few times a month.

What about Green Tripe (the other Green Meat)? Unwashed green tripe is a cow stomach, complete with the partially digested stomach contents. Not to be confused with the processed bleached tripe sold for human consumption — they use lye to clean it — green tripe has enzymes and beneficial bacteria galore. It is a great addition to the diet, though not a necessary component. This is often fed to zoo animals and racing greyhounds, and is more commonly fed in Europe than here. Some people swear by it. It can be hard to find, but there are suppliers who package it for dogs. If your local meat provider does not have a source, check the internet. Many of the frozen raw food purveyors in the Resource section carry green tripe.

Another simple way to feed organ meat is to add it to their veggie glop. Fido will find it makes his veggies ever so enticing.

The Fun Stuff...Veggie Glop

Fruits and vegetables provide important nutrients and fiber to keep Rover regular. Wild canids get these nutrients by eating the partially digested stomach contents of their prey that would include grasses and other vegetable matter — and other good things. They also get fiber by eating the fur/hair of their prey. Veggie glop is my version of what we humans can create that most closely approximates this part of the diet of the wild canid. You will need to pulverize fruits and veggies to help with this process. Pureeing and then freezing the vegetable matter and combining with the "other" items described in this chapter creates a nutritious veggie glop. Freezing the resulting glop serves two purposes: it further breaks down the cell walls of veggie matter to make the nutrients bio available and it allows for volume "manufacturing" of the raw food diet so that it is MUCH easier to manage. While freezing can cause a loss in the nutrients that will be available in the food, the loss is small or negligible. Tossing in the incidental cooked veggie is absolutely fine and indeed cooking squash, carrots, and tomatoes is the only way to make some of their nutrients bio available. Whenever I have the urge to start

Veggie glop is my version of what we humans can create that most closely approximates part of the diet of the wild canid.

micromanaging my dogs' diet, I remember these are animals that eat kitty bon-bons, polish off our Thai curry leftovers and don't mind eating bananas and garlic at the same time!

Vegetables. Dark green leafy veggies make up the bulk of the veggie component of the glop. Use any lettuce but iceberg (which is virtually nutrition-free), chard, mustard greens, parsley, and carrot tops. I try to make the green leafy portion of the glop about 50% of the total. If I happen to have a lot of green beans and squash, then that's what goes in. If I have a whole bag of Romaine lettuce, they get lots of that. Overall there's lots of variety, I think that's mainly what counts. Then I add orange, red or yellow veggies to assure a full range of nutrients. Carrots store well and dogs usually love them. I feed them both cooked and uncooked. Winter or summer squash, sweet potatoes, and pumpkin are good. If using pumpkin or any winter squash, I cook it first because it's so tough otherwise — and I add the seeds too. When I use sweet potatoes I can never figure out whether they "should" be raw or cooked. So I alternate. Sometimes they are cooked, sometimes raw.

Sometimes they are cooked, sometimes raw.

Green beans, asparagus stalks (I like the tips too much to share), peas, celery, radishes, cucumbers and other such vegetable are thrown in when available. Cabbage, cauliflower, kale and broccoli are included, though not in huge amounts as cruciferous vegetables can give the dogs gas and depress thyroid function if overfed. I also limit those from the nightshade family (eggplant, tomatoes, peppers, potatoes) because they can aggravate inflammatory conditions, especially in arthritic dogs. Raw potatoes should always be peeled, since the skins can be poisonous. If baked they can be fed skins and all. In fact, onions are the only vegetable I don't use. They can cause anemia in dogs.

FREE Greens. For a totally FREE and novel source of veggies, wild greens are a nutritional goldmine! I use lots of dandelion leaves because those are easy to identify. I also pick sage, mint, burdock, couch grass and pigweed. Just be sure they haven't been

treated with chemicals of any kind. Few wild plants are poisonous, but you should know what you are picking so, to be safe, get
a book on identifying edible wild greens.

Fruit. I use fruit too — my old dog refused to eat her veggies until I started adding bananas and garlic. The riper the better, but too
much fruit in the glop can cause diarrhea in some dogs. I've tried
almost every fruit known to humankind and find that as long as I
don't overdo it, the dogs will gobble it up in their glop.

Eggs contain essential fatty acids and are excellent for the skin and coat.

Eggs. Fed whole, these are perfect,
balanced protein for your dog. I add
them to the glop, shell and all. You
may have heard that raw egg whites
will prevent your dog from absorbing
biotin, a B vitamin, but not if you feed
them with the yolks. Eggs can also be quickly soft boiled, just
leave the yolks runny.

My dogs get 2-3 eggs a week each mixed in with their glop and
an additional one or two eggs a week because they just love them.
Some people feed eggs daily. Eggs contain essential fatty acids
and are excellent for the skin and coat. If you want to test your
dog's problem solving skills, see what she does with a whole
egg!

Dairy. Almost all dogs benefit from probiotic-rich yogurt. Made
from full fat, low fat, skim milk are all fine; unsweetened or naturally sweetened. Look for a notation on the container such as
"contains live bacteria cultures" or similar to be sure it contains
these useful probiotics. Add yogurt to glop or use it as a topping.
Freezing for as long as three months will kill only a minute per-
centage of the active cultures.

As for feeding your dog other dairy products, my research indicates that there are no major benefits in feeding dairy other than
yogurt. I don't go out of my way to feed it but if I have cottage
cheese or other dairy on hand, I add that to the glop. Cheddar and
other natural cheeses are TREATS at our house!

Apple Cider Vinegar. ACV is one of those folk remedies that have been around for literally thousands of years. It's credited with being a natural antibiotic, soothing arthritis symptoms, aiding digestion, lowering cholesterol, and Dog only knows what else! Be sure to use *unpasteurized* ACV to get friendly bacteria. I put a healthy splash into the glop.

Blackstrap Molasses. Blackstrap molasses adds a little sweetness that most dogs love without too much sugar. It's high in iron and vitamin B. I don't always use it often but a tablespoon or so in the mix is always appreciated.

Garlic, Ginger. Most dogs love garlic. That alone is a good enough reason to feed it — it's also supposed to be good for controlling parasites and fungus. Ginger is something I keep on hand for human cooking and the dogs certainly don't mind the taste. It is considered a good antioxidant. I don't think these are essential foods, but the canine pack enjoys a little seasoning too.

Most dogs love garlic.

Nuts and Legumes. Not a big part of what I feed, but sometimes I throw a handful of raw nuts, squash or melon seeds into the glop for the minerals and micronutrients. My dogs also love nuts as treats. Cooper will delicately shell pistachios to get to the meat. Nuts make good rewards for hide and seek games. Use them to see how good your dog is at sniffing out a single almond that you've placed on the floor in another room while he practices his down-stays!

I don't feed legumes (beans) other than those they may eat in our leftovers because they give my dogs gas. They don't add anything important to the diet because dogs poorly utilize the protein in beans.

Water

Add just enough water to your veggie glop ingredients to make your machine blend smoothly. Your dog will be getting lots of water in the raw foods you are feeding. You may be surprised at how her water consumption slows down.

Shhh...I Feed Some Grains

While I don't believe that any grain is absolutely essential for a dog, many dogs do fine with a little bit here and there. Cooper and Phoebe are my low-metabolism dogs so I sometimes give them a little boiled rice — usually brown — to fill them up. When I feed them "diet plate" meals sometimes I add a little soaked or cooked rolled oats: 1 tablespoon to 1/4 cup per quart of veggie glop. I spent many years growing up in Scotland around working Border Collies. A big part of the working collie diet is oatmeal, along with potatoes, raw fish, and table scraps. One of the most widely used commercial working-dog foods in Scotland is oatmeal based and looks like granola. These dogs work hard and rarely go to the vet. I guess I'm just being nostalgic — it makes me feel nurturing. This little divergence from the RMB and veggie diet shows you that I'm not a maniacal purist about how I feed my dogs. None of my dogs seem to have a problem with a little oatmeal or rice and, as grains go, they are quite nutritious.

Pizza crusts are referred to as pizza bones around here so pizza night is a treat for both dogs and humans.

If you decide to feed grains, be aware, not all grains agree with all dogs! I have found that more than a mere scrap of anything containing wheat flour or corn will give Cooper terrible gas. On the other hand, because Daphne is a huge eater and burns calories at an alarming rate, I sometimes give her a piece of whole wheat bread or a cup of cooked brown rice along with her dinner to fill her up. Whole grains take longer to digest than raw meat and bones and I find it keeps her better satisfied until her next meal. I wish I had her metabolism!

I have a friend with a Great Dane who had a terrible time keeping weight on her frame either on kibble or a grain-less raw diet. It was only when she started adding about a cup of cooked oatmeal to her evening meal that she was finally able to keep a good weight. Remember, a cup of cooked oats is a very small proportion of the whole diet for a 135 lb. dog. If you decide to feed grains, keep them as a small part of the diet.

Moo Goo Gai Pan and Pizza Bones. For as long as I've owned dogs, they have been allowed to clean select leftovers off our plates, and I see no reason to stop now. Pizza crusts are referred to as pizza bones around here so pizza night is a treat for both dogs and humans. If you want to toss some healthy leftovers into the glop, your dog will be happy to help you dispose of them.

Relax About Supplements

Whenever possible purchase natural rather than synthetic.

One of the things that intimidated me about this diet initially was reading long, detailed lists of what some people supplemented with on a daily basis. Discussions about whether powdered Icelandic kelp was better than Pacific kelp, or the proper temperature to store flax seed oil, or what vital nutrient would be missing if one fed Brand A fish oil versus Brand B didn't help one bit! Once I realized the huge array of bio-available nutrients supplied by the raw foods alone, I relaxed and started to apply some common sense to supplementation.

I use supplements in moderation to be sure I am covering all the nutritional bases. Most of my dogs take whole fish oil and E gel caps readily like treats. I use ground meat for Phoebe's supplements, making up a couple of days worth of little supplement-filled meatballs at a time. I feed all supplements with their meals.

For the supplements I do use I buy house brand, human supplements rather than pricier, boutique-y types and find they work just as well. Whenever possible I purchase natural rather than synthetic. One caution: don't use one of those canine vitamin/mineral all-in-one supplements, especially with a growing puppy — at least not until checking out a particular brand carefully. Many contain calcium, and you don't want to overdo that because it can cause joint problems with growing puppies.

Certain health issues, like Phoebe's arthritis, may warrant extras. She gets added glucosamine/chondroitin with MSM with her evening meal and it works well to relieve pain. But remember: there is an incredible array of beautifully balanced nutrients in a fresh raw diet. The diet alone provides a wealth of nutrients and unlike commercial food and supplements; they are fresh and easily assimilated. Do not be tempted to overdo supplements, you can actually do harm by feeding too many added artificial vitamins and minerals.

Just know that you do not *have* to give your dog 59 vitamins a day. Many raw feeders use none at all. There are numerous books with a wealth of information on vitamins and supplements (see Resources). I'll just explain what I supplement with and why.

Supplements I Use and Why

Fish oil. I give my dogs fish oil gel caps 3 to 4 times a week. The dogs think these are treats and come running at the sound of the pill bottle rattling. Fish oils are an important source of essential fatty acids (EFA's), particularly Omega-3, in the diet. This balances out the Omega-6 fatty acids found in abundance in raw animal fat. While some raw feeders use flax seed oil as a source of Omega-3 some dogs are sensitive to it and get itchy skin so I stick with fish oil.

Remember, "balance over time!"

For my large dogs, I give them the human dose of one, 1000 mg capsule each about four times a week. Figure roughly 100-300 mg per 10 lbs. of dog although I've seen higher doses recommended. People with smaller dogs can poke a hole in the capsule and put a drop or two or four on Buster's food. It's difficult to overdose, so don't sweat exact amounts.

Vitamin E. My dogs get Vitamin E regularly along with the fish oil; they eat these whole like treats. It's a major antioxidant and good for their hearts. Phoebe has had a heart murmur and erratic heartbeat for several years, but is asymptomatic. She gets 1000 mg of E at least three times a week.

A good rule of thumb is to give between 50-100 I.U.s per 10 lbs. of dog. Since it often comes in 400 I.U. gel caps, you can give 400

I.U. on Monday and 1200 I.U. on Wednesday. I figure it evens out over time. Remember, "balance over time!"

Vitamin C. While dogs produce their own Vitamin C, it's not always enough to help their systems deal with physical or emotional stress and general pollutants. Vitamin C is an excellent antioxidant and large doses of C have been found in several studies to reduce symptoms of hip dysplasia and joint problems, especially in larger breeds.

A simple rule of thumb is to supplement with 250-500 mg per day for every 10 lbs. of dog. I add it to the glop when I make it so the dosage is divided between meals by "guesstimating" how much each portion will be. Be sure you introduce Vitamin C gradually because too much, too soon may result in diarrhea. Start with just a scant amount, like a pinch of powder added to the meal, and increase the amount slowly over a month or so.

The most common (and cheapest) form of Vitamin C is ascorbic acid, however, it is not well assimilated by dogs and can irritate their stomachs. I suggest you purchase a formula that uses either calcium ascorbate or sodium ascorbate.

Glucosamine/chondroitin/MSM. Per my vet, Phoebe gets 1500 mg of glucosamine and 1200 mg of chondroitin daily for arthritis. These definitely make a difference in her level of mobility. If I skip a couple of days she gets creakier. I also give her 800 mg of MSM (methyl-sulfonyl-methane) daily. This has been shown in a number of studies to ease arthritic pain and swelling in both dogs and people. It's a naturally occurring dietary sulphur and has no negative side effects.

CHAPTER 5

The Raw Food Factory

I believe that the only practical way to make a long-term commitment to the raw dog food diet is to devise a *system* that makes it easy to both make the food and to feed it. By having the right tools to do the job, finding reliable and economical sources for the ingredients, and having an efficient "manufacturing" and storage system, it will become second nature for you to make your dog's food. When you have these things in place feeding raw is a cinch!

The Tools Of The Trade

So, do you need any special kitchen equipment? You probably have what you need already. Here's a quick checklist:

Knives. I use a very sharp knife if I have to cut things up. A friend gave me one of those "As Seen On TV" knives and I have to say it does a great job of cutting up whole chickens and large pieces of pork neck. I also have a cleaver to cut the larger turkey necks into 6" lengths. A knife sharpener is a handy thing to have on hand. It's amazing how much easier cutting through gristle and raw meat is when you have a high quality, sharp knife. Since my dogs are big, I don't have to do much chopping so not much labor involved here.

Cutting Board. Use a good quality plastic or hardwood board. Plastic should be dishwasher safe and washed after each use; you can sanitize your wooden board after each use with a weak bleach solution of 1 tablespoon bleach to 1 gallon water.

Food Processor.
For gloperizing, I
have a VitaMix™
blender. I adore it.
This thing will re-
duce almost any-
thing to paste with-
in 60 seconds. It was
a gift. I don't think I
would have bought
such a pricey ma-
chine ($300-800 de-

pending on model) for myself. Any kitchen machine that thoroughly pulps vegetables will work—food processors, juicers or
small grinders will all do the trick. A word about using blend-
ers: most seem to need lots of liquid in order to puree the vegetable matter so you will need to feed more if you've processed your
glop this way.

Storage Containers. Meat that is purchased in shrink-
wrapped styrofoam trays is simply frozen in the original wrap-
ping. When I thaw them, there is usually enough to feed my pack
for 1-3 days at a time. When RMBs come in bulk, I separate them
into more manageable units (again 1-3 days supply), and I either
double-wrap them in grocery bags, or put in zip-lock baggies. For
true convenience spread the RMBs on baking sheets, allow them
to freeze solid and then bag them up. Then you can pull them out
one at a time.

The glop I make is invariably stored in 1 lb. yogurt tubs since
I have plenty of these. Some raw feeders favor zip lock freezer bags. They have the advantage of allowing you to freeze
the glop flat and stacking the bags to save on freezer space.
Small dog owners can pour the glop into ice-cube trays, freeze,
pop the cubes out and bag them. Small yogurt cups with lids
are good for little veggie-meals too. Any number of food-
saver type containers will work; use the appropriate size so
that you thaw enough for no more than 1-3 days at a time.

Refrigerator and Freezer Space. The bottom shelf of my fridge is the dog-shelf. I use a large plastic container, big enough to hold thawing RMBs, meat and veggie glop for about three days of food for my herd of dogs. It catches any drips from thawing food. In between uses I clean it with a mild bleach solution to keep it sanitary.

Do you *need* a whole separate freezer to manage the raw food diet? You really don't have to, especially if you have a smaller dog or are just starting out. Just be sure you have enough freezer space to take advantage of bulk buys and sales and for storage of your veggie glop.

You probably already have the kitchen equipment you'll need.

A few hints if you decide to go freezer shopping:

Get a much larger one than you think you will need! Trust me, you'll use the space—if not for Fluffy's RMBs, for extra stocks of biped food. I *thought* I had bought a large enough freezer when I bought mine but haven't been able to take advantage of some excellent deals because space is lacking.

Resist the temptation to get a cheap, used, elderly freezer. The savings you make on the purchase price can easily be negated in a single year's worth of higher energy bills. I bought a "scratch and dent" floor model for a very reasonable price, and it's extremely energy efficient.

Consider purchasing an upright freezer because they are easier to organize. I have to practically stand on my head to reach the bottom of my chest freezer, and things get very jumbled in there. Wish I'd bought an upright! Plus the chest freezers take up more room.

Things I don't use but other people swear by:

Dehydrator: Many people use make their own dog treats, or dehydrate meat for traveling, vacations, and such. Remember, even the relatively low heat of a dehydrator cooks the food so some of the benefit of feeding raw disappears, but at least you are able to control the ingredients.

Meat grinder: These don't have to be expensive, it depends what sorts of RMBs you want to grind. For about $100, you can get a grinder that will handily grind chicken, fish, and small pork or lamb bones. They can be used to grind meat and vegetables together too. If you want to grind larger bones, whole poultry carcasses, or large amounts in a short while, look into a higher capacity grinder. If you don't want to or can't feed RMBs, this is how to get the nutritional benefit of RMBs without actually feeding whole meaty bones to your dog.

Vacuum sealer.

Scales for weighing portions.

Measuring spoons and cups.

Kitchen shears.

If you want to grind larger bones, whole poultry carcasses, or large amounts in a short while, look into a higher capacity grinder.

Coffee grinder for grinding eggshells, pills, seeds.

Rubber or latex gloves keep gunk out from under fingernails; filet gloves, reinforced with metal to protect hands if you are an over-zealous chopper and risk cutting off a digit or two.

Garlic press for squeezing liquid out of gel caps or even for squishing small chunks of softer veggies.

Let's hunt, gather and freeze!

For many people, like me, finding great deals can become quite a pastime. It's even improved my social life! I've made friends in the meat packing industry, found some really interesting little foreign food markets, and met nice people through a local on-line raw feeding supplier group.

Here is how I "hunt and gather" ingredients:

Chasing Chickens...Sources for Meat. Aside from the obvious — your local supermarket and bulk food warehouse —

get out your phone book and look under "meat, wholesale and retail." In most states you can buy directly from meat wholesalers. You may have to buy in 30-40 lb. cases, but if you've got a pack of hearty eaters and plenty of freezer space, it is a great way to go.

Check with favorite restaurants. You may find one that will order extra cases of meat for you.

If you live in a city, try ethnic markets. You can find animal parts you didn't know existed! I buy cheap organic chicken feet from a Chinese market. If nothing else, the entertainment value of watching the dogs eat them little toes is worth a buck a pound! The storeowner does not know I buy these for the dogs and has given me chicken foot recipes. I'm starting to feel a bit guilty!

Watch for sales. Even large drug store chains, the kind that have a couple of food aisles, can be a good resource. I've gotten some incredible deals on bulk buys of canned salmon and mackerel.

Check the newspaper for organic meat suppliers. Join on-line supplier groups or search the internet for small ranches or farms that do their own processing (see Resources). I have gotten free freezer-burned emu meat, venison, and buffalo this way. If you're in hunting country, put the word out that you will take deer leftovers. Some people pick up road-killed game but check with your local highway department to make sure it is legal and safe in your area.

Meat Storage Solutions. If you purchase your meat in those handy-dandy shrink-wrapped trays in relatively small units, you can just toss them straight into the freezer and defrost them as needed. If you think you are going to leave it frozen for months and months, you can rewrap it in freezer paper to avoid freezer burn, though honestly it won't make any difference to your dogs!

If you purchase a rack of beef, pork, or lamb rib bones, you may want to cut them apart and then freeze them in smaller proportions so you can take them out as needed.

Most dogs are fine with partially or even completely frozen raw meaty bones!

If your meat comes in a 40 lb. frozen solid block as mine often does, you can thaw it out in a sink full of cold water. I use the laundry room sink for this. As it defrosts from the outside in, I pry off and bag pieces before it completely defrosts and into the freezer it goes. Another way to do it (endorsed by my butcher) is to drop the 40 lb. wad of meat onto a hard surface, concrete for example, as hard as you can. This breaks up the ice that holds the pieces together and you can bag it up without defrosting.

Some friends of mine with two very large dogs have sweet-talked their neighborhood supermarket into keeping their cases of chicken parts, purchased at the market on special, in the butcher's cold storage. They can drop by and pick up just enough for a few days at a time. Many people bag up just one day's worth, and take them out a day ahead of time to defrost in a plastic bin in the fridge. Most dogs are fine with partially or even completely frozen RMBs. It is a great way to get an aggressive eater to slow down. And, for those times when you forget to defrost something, keep some canned fish on hand.

Don't try these at home! Some inventive ways of breaking up frozen RMBs I've actually tried that do NOT work:

> Driving over turkey necks with a pick up truck. At best, they will be partially crushed, but not only is this tricky to do in your driveway, you need a bit of speed to go over a 40 lb. block of frozen turkey necks, you risk grinding asphalt chips into the meat. This is Not Good.

> Putting very large raw fish between boards (so you don't get fish slime in your tire treads) and driving over them fast. This causes high velocity fish pieces to shoot into neighboring counties.

Reciprocating saws, band saws, table saws, chainsaw massa-
cring of large things like turkey necks is also not recommended. It does work, but it's overkill and messy.

Greens Grazing...Sources for Vegetables, etc.

At the store, I buy what's in season and inexpensive. When I buy
radishes, carrots, etc. I choose those with their green tops intact.
Then all the trimmings—greens, broccoli stems, melon seeds,
wilted lettuce, limp carrots—go into my glop.

Find a nearby juice bar and arrange to pick up their pulp. There is still a gold mine of nutrition left in the pulp!

Make friends with the produce manag-
er. Ask about blemished, old and wilted fruits and veggies and always check
sale bins. You may be able to get the
store to set aside produce for you instead of throwing it away. I'm not sug-
gesting you feed spoiled, rotten produce. It's just that the public
rejects perfectly good food because it isn't cosmetically perfect,
and that may mean a bargain for you.

Farmers markets are a great place to stock up and the produce you
buy there is often organic. Keep independent farmers working!
There may be great buys at the end of the day if you are buying in
bulk. If you are pinching pennies you may want to try dumpster
diving. Some vendors will simply throw away perfectly good un-
sold produce rather than truck it back to the farm where it will go
to waste anyway.

Grow your own vegetables. I have a vegetable garden every year
as well as using wild greens from my property. Both are organic
and pesticide free. Veggie glop is the perfect way to use up that
baseball bat sized zucchini!

Find a nearby juice bar and arrange to pick up their pulp. There is
still a goldmine of nutrition left in the pulp.

The freezer is your best friend when grazing for greens and stor-
ing a bumper crop of ingredients. I keep an empty container in the
freezer and toss in healthy trimmings until I get around to making my next batch of veggie glop. It seems nothing goes to waste
at our house.

CHAPTER 6

Putting It All Together

OK! You're ready to start serving Rover his New! Improved! Back to Nature! REAL! RAW! **FOOD!**

Making the Switch is Easy

Want to know how easy it is to switch diets? Next time you're at the grocery store, pick up a package of chicken wings, backs or necks. This is the easiest meat for most dogs to digest. Even a tiny dog can handle a chicken neck or smashed up chicken back. You'd be surprised! Just avoid the larger weight bearing bones like drumsticks at first.

Let your dog miss one meal. Feed your dog a piece of raw chicken, bones and all (if the piece is especially fatty, remove some of it). There. You've done it! You're feeding Raw. It's really that easy.

When starting out, feed one type of RMBs, usually chicken and nothing else for at least a week. Some people start with a good commercially prepared raw ground product, and then start adding whole RMBs and other ingredi-

ents later on. While I have never done this and don't feel it's necessary, if it increases your comfort level, by all means give it a try. Phasing out kibble gradually isn't necessary and may not work very well. Many times a dog will eat the good stuff—the raw food —and start refusing the kibble. Guess they know what's good for them. Missing a meal will ensure that the stomach is pretty empty and your dog will be hungry enough to try something different.

What if he doesn't have a clue that this is FOOD? I haven't had a single dog turn down raw meaty bones, but some dogs don't get the concept that RMBs are actually a food item. My friend's Rottie, Casey, thought chicken backs were for licking, nuzzling, playing with and burying. But eating? Heavens no. How absolutely barbaric! Ladies just don't do that. It took her awhile to get a clue. Later on I'll address solutions to common and not-so-common problems.

Then the Veggie Glop

Forget about supplements for the first few weeks.

After the weeklong introduction of RMBs you can slowly start adding a simplified version of the veggie glop to the diet. Keep it simple at first. Try one or two green leafy vegetables combined with summer or winter squash, some plain yogurt, and some canned fish or ground meat to make it tastier. Forget about supplements for the first few weeks. Wait until Fifi is eating and processing her food without a hitch.

Start with a teaspoon or two per meal for a small dog; a tablespoon or two for a big one and see how your dog tolerates it. Over the course of the next few weeks, you can add a bit more glop and more variety. As with any change in diet, some initial diarrhea may occur. If your dog seems otherwise fine and the diarrhea isn't terribly runny or doesn't last for more than a couple of days, don't worry about it. Just review what you are feeding to determine if you've added something new that you may need to eliminate for now. There's a complete veggie glop "recipe" at the end of this chapter.

Really, that is it. After a while, you will settle into a routine for producing and feeding a raw foods diet. You will become comfortable with going by what is convenient for you, what foods your dog does well on and what's in season and inexpensive. Have fun with it!

How Much to Feed

As with kibble feeding instructions, the guidelines for feeding raw are just that—rough guidelines. Dogs have different metabolic rates and activity levels. You would expect the nutritional needs for a working Border Collie to be somewhat greater than that of an elderly Basset Hound. You probably already have an idea of her general food requirements. You know whether she eats the higher recommended kibble amounts without gaining weight, what her activity level is, or if she needs to lose or gain weight. If you are not sure if she's at an ideal weight, have your vet check her condition. Weigh her while she's at the vet's, and weigh her periodically to see how she is doing. In between times I use the "rib-feel" technique. You should always be able to feel a thin covering of fat covering her ribs.

A good rule of thumb is feeding 2-3% of the dog's ideal weight per day, in total food intake.

A good rule of thumb is feeding **2-3% of the dog's ideal weight per day**, in total food intake. Say Trixie is a moderately active 60 lbs. but her ideal weight is 50 lbs. You would want to feed her 2% of 50 lbs., which is 1 lb. daily. An inexpensive kitchen scale will help you. I didn't have one and overfed Phoebe when I first started. She gained seven unwanted pounds, and it took months to get her weight down. I will warn you! An old dog with a slow metabolism will lose weight at a glacially slow rate.

I feed my dogs 20-25%, by volume, of veggie glop by simply "eyeballing" it. They get veggie glop every day. I find that too much at once doesn't get eaten and may cause loose stools. Some people do well feeding just a few "all veggie" meals a week. Some folk feed more vegetables, some less, some never feed veggies. Do your own "field testing" and find what out what works for you and your dog.

Now here are the caveats to that rule of thumb!

First, small dogs have higher metabolisms. Little, active dogs could need to eat as much as 10% of their weight.

The type of food you feed also makes a difference.

A large, slow moving dog may need less than 2%.

Dogs who spend time outside in cold weather will burn more calories than dogs who spend lots of time inside where it's warm, even with the same activity level.

If you have more than one dog, they are likely playing and moving around during the day, and could need more food than the home-alone guy who waits for you to come home.

The type of food you feed also makes a difference. If your dog gets lots of chicken backs that are usually quite fatty, they will need less than if they eat more turkey necks or rabbit meat that are fairly lean meats.

Are you starting to see why it's difficult for me to tell you how much you should be feeding *your* dog?

How often to feed?

I feed my dogs twice a day. Smaller dogs usually have a faster metabolism and an empty stomach can make them throw up bile. Large, deep-chested dogs can be more prone to bloat and feeding twice a day helps prevent this. Of course, many people feed once a day and their dogs are absolutely fine with that. My mother's Border Collie only eats in the evening, and I only started a two meal per day regimen after I started owning Rottweilers and learned about bloat. Hey, dogs love to eat, so why deny them such pleasure? Just keep the meals small and don't overfeed.

Here's What My Dogs Eat

To review: My dog pack includes Daphne, a small, lithe adult Rottweiler who weighs only 70 lbs. She's an energetic jumping bean who won't walk if she can run. This little blast furnace eats

2-3 lbs. of food a day, easily 3% of her weight. Cooper is a 100 lb. adolescent and still has a little growing to do. He is a very laid back gentleman and it takes very little extra food for him to gain weight. By conserving every calorie I'm sure he will outlast everyone in a famine! Cooper eats 1-2 lbs. a day; less than 2% of his weight. Despite their size differences and due to their differing energy levels and metabolisms Cooper eats less than Daphne. 100 lb. Dutch only eats until he's full. He has a built in appestat, lucky guy, and maintains his weight on 2 lbs. of food a day—2% of his weight. Phoebe is a little less than 80 lbs. and quite inactive due to her advanced age. She gets the same diet as the others but with fewer RMBs. I give her about 1 lb. of food a day—that is less than 2% of her weight.

Morning meal per dog. RMBs—beef ribs, chicken parts, turkey necks, rabbit, whatever I have on hand. Since there is such a wide range in RMB sizes, I will leave it up to you to figure amounts! For instance, chicken backs can weigh anywhere from 3 oz. to 1 lb. each. A slab of beef ribs may be a light meal for most dogs—unless you have a super-duper power chewer who can eat all the ribs up too—most dogs will just eat the meat.

Just get close to the suggested quantities and don't break your equipment.

Evening meal per dog. I give 1/2 to 1 cup of the veggie glop along with a little more RMBs or one of the following: 1/2 lb. of whole or ground meat, canned fish or raw smelt, a slice of beef liver, pork steak, heart, etc. On the occasions that I give them soaked oatmeal or cooked sweet potato, this is when they get it. If they've had a lazy day, or look like they need to drop a pound or so, I forgo meat and just add the grains or cooked sweet potato. For fussy eaters I make the veggie glop more attractive by drizzling a little of the watery blood from the thawing meat in the fridge over it. While many people feed veggies just a few days per week and that works just fine for them, my younger dogs tend to get diarrhea if they get too much glop at one time. I space it out daily.

Balance over time. Does anybody out there achieve "complete balanced nutrition" within each meal? I very much doubt it. Since I feed four large dogs, I make a point of stocking up whenever I find sales; therefore what I feed varies from month to month depending on supplies. I belong to a regional online raw feeding group, and we alert each other to local sales. Because of cost I generally feed canned mackerel, not salmon. But word came through the grapevine that a local big box store had a sale on canned salmon for the same price as mackerel so I stocked up. When a supermarket chain had ground turkey on sale for .33/lb. a few weeks ago I stockpiled that and when they had chicken leg quarters on sale for .29/lb. I bought a quantity of those. Today I traded some tripe for some pork shoulder blades from one of the trainers where I take my dogs, so tonight's dinner was fresh meaty pork bones and a handful of chicken gizzards. So you can be flexible in your meal planning, seek variety and you will achieve balance over time. See the Resources section for a sample weeklong feeding diary. You can tell that I have fun finding new taste treats for my gang by the range of meats I feed. You DO NOT have to be that varied—unless you turn into a raw feeding geek like me!

From soup to spackle...a flexible glop recipe.

Now, I'm going to give you my "recipe" for veggie glop, however you have to promise me that you won't take this too seriously. It's not like you're baking a soufflé or something. Just get close to the suggested quantities and don't break your equipment. If you roughly chop your greens, fruits and veggies before processing, you'll be good to go.

The following is per batch. Most processors have a 4-6 cup capacity. Experiment as you go and for heaven's sake have FUN. OK?

Liquid Base

A couple of whole raw eggs, with shell

About 1/2 cup yogurt

Splash of apple cider vinegar—about a quarter of a cup

Tablespoon of black strap molasses

Teaspoon of powdered vitamin C

Adding the veggies. To this I add as much vegetable matter as possible—1-2 lbs. of veggies, depending on what type and consistency. Rinse the fruit and vegetables as needed. Pre-chop anything you think might jam up your machine. No need to peel — except the obvious ones like bananas. Use up those tough broccoli stalks, carrot tops, beet tops, overgrown zucchini etc. Toss in as many greens as will fit in there, along with squash, fruit, yams, celery, whatever. Couple of garlic cloves, sometimes a little gingerroot—many dogs love the taste! It's yet another ingredient I usually have on hand anyhow for biped cooking. Keep adding these to the liquid base until you've reached a good consistency—and capacity. Add water as needed to help liquefy the glop. You can also use the "juice" from defrosting RMBs if you have it on hand. It will make even the reluctant veggie eater happy to scarf down those greens. Put in juicier fruits or veggies (like apples, pears, berries or squash) first to make blending the tougher things like chopped greens easier. Pour into containers and freeze. That's it.

You can also use the "juice" from defrosting RMBs if you have it on hand.

A month's worth in an hour. I can make a month's worth of veggie glop for my four-pack in an hour as long as I have ingredients and enough containers on hand. I have fun using clear plastic deli tubs so I can make festive layers of pretty colors with different ingredients! The addition of a small beet will make it a really hot fuchsia color, while red peppers and carrots complement the greens well. (Do I know how to have a good time or what?)

To make your glop more "attractive" to a finicky canine gourmand you can add organ meats, ground meat or canned fish to the glop.

Doggie Dining Room

Since the boys can't be fed together, one always eats inside on the old washable throw rug in the kitchen. Otherwise, I feed my dogs in the garage where there are large pieces of carpet remnants that I just replace as needed. They can also go from the garage out to the yard if they prefer dining *al fresco* which is what usually happens with RMBs.

I use stainless steel bowls for all their food. They are very easy to clean. Plastic can harbor bacteria and other nasties, even with cleaning. Besides, my dogs will rip plastic bowls to shreds just for fun.

CHAPTER 7

Customize Your Feeding

Puppies

What if you have a puppy? Simple. More frequent feedings of the same basic adult diet, in the same proportions. I am too horrible with arithmetic to keep recalculating food weight and there were weeks when puppy Cooper gained 5 lbs., others where he would gain nothing. I just fed him as much as he would eat in 5-10 minutes.

If you're a mathematical type and prefer to feed by percentages of your pup's weight, here are the rules of thumb: Either feed 2-3% of the expected adult weight, or between 5% and 10% of your pup's current weight. Don't just go by numbers, though. Go by how your pup looks and feels. To ensure that your pup is well fed you should always be able to feel a thin covering of fat covering her ribs.

If you bring home an 8-week-old puppy, start by feeding him 3-4 times per day for the first month or so. Take the total daily amount of food that you calculated for the pup and divide it into 3-4 portions and feed throughout the day. Smaller meals are better. Don't let him gorge himself into a coma at each feeding. Occasionally a puppy will voluntarily skip a meal and as long as it's infrequent, don't worry. This could be just a sign that he's ready to go to fewer daily feedings. If, however, your puppy does not want to eat for an entire day, please consult your vet.

Feed as wide a variety of different meat types as possible. Toy breed puppies can eat chicken wing tips and chicken back pieces.

Don't let those itsy bitsy jaws fool you! Inside that little Chihua-hua or Yorkie beats the heart of a timber wolf. The little guys can demolish smaller RMBs quite handily. Many people grind much of their toy dog's RMBs, or they buy some commercially prepared raw food to ensure they get a good variety. Some small puppies do better if the RMBs are smashed into smaller pieces with a ham-mer first. And don't forget to make sure your pup has a good rec-reational bone to chew on and exercise those teeth and jaws. Try a chicken foot for a fun meal, if you can find them.

Small breed puppies that mature faster should be ready to start twice a day feedings by about 4-5 months old; large breed pups by 7-8 months of age. Raw meal frequency is no different than kib-ble meal frequency. I think that twice a day feeding for life is best. Very large dogs will continue to grow until at least three years old and some dogs, especially toy breeds, can get an upset tummy and may vomit bile from an empty stomach if they're only fed once every 24 hours.

Rescues and Fosters...Too Skinny

I feed rescues and fosters the same diet as my other dogs, start-ing out slowly with lean meaty chicken, bones and all, adding more fat as tolerated. A drizzle of olive oil, pat of butter, nuts, pork hocks, extra chicken skin for the skinny ones will help put on the weight. Work up to more and more fat as tolerated by the dog. If you see stools loosening, then back off the fat. You might want to increase RMBs for skinny dogs, too. The marrow contains fat and other nutrients.

A drizzle of olive oil, pat of butter, nuts, pork hocks, extra chicken skin for the skinny ones will help put on the weight.

I start out on raw foods as described earlier. Nothing but chicken for up to a week, then slowly adding other ingredients until they are used to it. Apart from "pudding poops" for a few days, I haven't had a dog take longer than about two seconds to figure out that they loved eating this way.

A friend offered this recipe for underweight dogs—to be fed as an in-between-meals snack for putting weight on. Mix two cups of soaked oat flakes, 1/2 cup of peanut butter, a banana and a healthy drizzle of olive oil. She fed this daily to her underweight Great Dane and swears by it for bulking up a skinny dog.

Rescues and Fosters...Too Fat

What if the dog needs to lose excess weight? Simple, feed just as if *you* were trying to lose weight! Feed leaner RMBs like turkey necks, fish or rabbit. Cut back on the total food volume and learn to ignore pleading eyes. A nice chew bone will help take Chubby's mind off impending starvation, too. And don't forget exercise and playing to get that metabolism going!

What should you do if you know that a foster dog will be put on kibble after re-homing? Well, since the dogs I've switched did so dramatically better shortly after switching diets, I figured even a month or two of real food would do some good.

Active Dogs

Since dogs get their energy primarily from animal protein and fats, feed your agility queen or jumping bean dog precisely that! My Daphne is very active. She's the type of dog who just vibrates in place when told to "down-stay." As I'm handing out the morning meat meal, I'll toss her the fattier pieces. She has boundless energy, her coat gleams, and when she runs I can see all her muscles rippling.

Small Dogs

Small dogs tend to have faster metabolisms than the big lumbering dogs, and may require as much as 10% of their body weight in daily food. Monitor and know your dog. Be aware of what a lean, healthy dog should look and feel like, and adjust meals accordingly. This is really no different than kibble feeding requirements. I

rarely fed any of my dogs what the feeding directions suggested when I fed kibble either. They were just suggestions, not commandments!

Small dogs seem to do better when fed twice a day through adulthood. Some toy dogs have more dental problems than larger dogs. If you are feeding primarily ground RMBs, make sure your little guy has recreational bones to chew on regularly! If your dog is a little, active terrier type, a hearty big chew bone can help her while away the time while she fantasizes about digging for mice and hunting rats.

Large Dogs

Compared to smaller breeds, large dogs often eat less for their body weight, especially if they are relatively inactive. No dog should be allowed to get overweight and large breeds can have even more joint problems if they're carrying around a spare tire. You can't really hurt your dog by underfeeding a little, but you can hurt her by a little overfeeding! Keep her lean—don't get beguiled by that "Oh mommy! I am so vewwy hungry" expression.

Larger RMBs are great for big dogs. They give a little more of a chewing workout, which seems more satisfying than meals that get gulped in six seconds.

Large deep-chested dogs are more prone to bloat and many believe a grain-free diet can help prevent this often deadly and very painful condition. Although bloat is perhaps less of a concern for dogs on raw foods, I still take the precaution of not feeding my dogs shortly after they've had lots of vigorous exercise. And if they've helped take care of some leftovers, I compensate by feeding a little less that day. Two small meals may be better than one large one. Try anything that will prevent your dog from inhaling lots of air as she eats. Keeping some large breeds lean can be a challenge. Rottweilers are walking stomachs and most would probably eat until they explode, given the chance.

Senior Citizens

Your aging dog will usually need less food to compensate for lowered activity levels. If his walks are less frequent and shorter, and he starts spending more time napping, back off his food

Diet might not be a cure-all, but can help with the health of all major organs and functions.

a little. Again (do you see a trend here, hmmm?) don't let him get overweight! A dog with stiff, aging joints will feel even worse carrying around extra fat.

Pay attention to how he chews, in case of dental problems, especially if he's been fed kibble most of his life. Unwillingness to chew, chewing with only one side of his mouth, drooling, or frequent runny eyes or nose can signal painful teeth or gums. Some people — I've seen this with Phoebe — notice their old dog is more likely to get constipated. Since RMBs alone can cause harder, drier poops, I make sure she gets a few extra veggies every day, and small amounts of organ meat frequently too. Hopefully you have a good relationship with your veterinarian so you can stay on top of any emerging health issues with your aging dog. Diet might not be a cure-all, but can help with the health of all major organs and functions.

Just the two of you or a whole pack?

If you are a single dog household, you will follow the same ingredient and production instructions as the multi dog family — just on a smaller scale. Or, better yet, you can make enough food to last 3 or 4 months in the same time it takes big and multi dog families to make a two-month supply. Lucky you! You'll probably find the space to store your canine cuisine alongside yours in the freezer if you don't buy or prepare in bulk...unless your dog is a Neapolitan Mastiff or something. Since I have four large dogs to feed, I do things on a larger scale, including having a "doggie" freezer. OK, sometimes the biped overflow gets in there too.

Other Feeding Concerns

Pregnancy, lactation, cancer, feeding under these circumstances is a level of complexity I really don't have the ability to address. I suggest seeking out more information from the books noted in the Resources section and looking for websites dealing with these issues. Hopefully you have a vet who is comfortable and knowledgeable about this diet—if not, find one who is, or consult with a canine nutritionist who can work with your dog and you.

CHAPTER 8

Problem Solving

Your dog (or you) may run into problems or have questions while making the switch to raw foods. Here are some common issues and possible solutions. If, no matter what you do, your dog isn't doing well or health-threatening symptoms persist, consult your vet. A dog that has watery diarrhea for three or more days, seems to have a tender stomach, is lethargic, or dehydrated should be seen by your veterinarian.

What! Me, eat RAW meat?

Puppies almost invariably take to this diet immediately, but some adult dogs may be picky. In the unlikely event that your dog seems to hesitate in the presence of Real Food, here are some ways to get a reluctant meat-eater to eat RMBs with gusto…

- Hold one end and play a little game of tug of war with it. Get him excited, use happy talk, and pretend to eat some yourself. Anything to get him to understand this is fun food.

- Warm it up. Do NOT do this in the microwave — it cooks from the inside out and the bones will start cooking. Put a little oil in a pan, very quickly sear the chicken, make sure it's not too hot, and offer it again. Try adding a little garlic powder or Parmesan cheese to the oil. Warm meat will smell much stronger to him. You can also run it under hot water to release the aroma.

- Smash or grind the RMBs up, or chop them into smaller chunks at first.

- Add a little lean ground meat. If he's reluctant, cook it a little first. As time goes on, you can back off on the cooking and feed it raw.

- Rub it with anything your dog likes. Garlic, Parmesan cheese, honey, bouillon powder.

- I've even heard of people putting some canned dog food on it, if you can stand the smell.

- Try another type of meat—if you've been offering chicken, try a pork neck or hunk of chuck roast instead.

- If your dogs lie around like hairy drooling speed bumps while you're working in the kitchen waiting for you to drop something edible (mine do this), put the RMB on the counter. Let it sit there in plain view and make sure he sees it. Finally offer it to him with a flourish and a happy voice—he might go for it! In the past, I've "tricked" dogs into taking pills like this: get them all worked up and convinced it's a treat, then toss it in the air. They'll often gulp it down without realizing the difference.

"Trick" dogs into taking pills...get them all worked up and convince them it's a treat, then toss it in the air!

- If your dogs are allowed to spit-polish your dinner plates after you've done eating, put a RMB on your plate and put it down as usual. A variation on the above trick, this can work. Finally, don't be afraid to let him miss a meal or two. He may just be mulling his options—if he realizes his options are "eat this weird thing" or "go hungry" he may well decide to just eat it.

- Some dogs will eat boneless meat without hesitation, but won't eat RMBs. So just feed boneless meat for the first several days and start adding a little bone-in meat gradually, perhaps a smashed up chicken wing nestled in a bed of ground chicken.

Yuck! Ick! Ptooie! – *Vegetables?*

Many dogs are reluctant to eat veggies at first. Perhaps I've been blessed; I've never had a dog hesitate much with these either. But you can try the following...

- Sweet tooth? Try adding a little fruit yogurt or honey — you can phase this out later.

- Add smelly, meaty things: defrosting juices from the meat, ground meats, canned fish, grated cheese. Heck! Add a little canned dog food or canned beef stew if that works. Again, you can phase it out over time.

- Smear the glop over the RMBs or meat.

- Try tricking him into thinking it's precious "people food" as above. Use your best china if you want.

- If he willingly eats canned fish or ground meat, mix in veggies in incrementally larger proportions until he's eating mostly or all glop.

- Add eggs — either lightly scrambled or raw.

Digestive Distress

Diarrhea is fairly common when doing any sort of diet switch, even switching brands of kibble. Of the dogs that I've switched to raw, only one had loose stools off and on for several weeks. The others were just fine as long as I kept it simple to begin with — RMBs, then one or two veggies and a little yogurt, and perhaps a little fruit. Many people use probiotics to boost the "good" bacteria in the gut, and/or digestive enzymes to help with moving things through the digestive tract at an appropriate speed. You can use those sold at natural food stores or better pet supply stores, adjusting the amounts to your dog's weight.

Recreational bones can be a temporary cause of loose stools because marrow is quite rich. When introducing RMBs for chewing I let the dog chew for an hour or so, then put it away in the fridge or freezer, then put it out the next day for slightly longer and so on to avoid their over-indulging.

> *Recreational bones can be a temporary cause of loose stools because marrow is quite rich.*

If the diarrhea is bad, or persists more than a few days and your vet gives her a clean bill of health, feed your dog some canned or cooked pumpkin a few times a day. Several tablespoons each feeding for a medium sized dog—mix it with something tasty. It does a wonderful job of absorbing water from the colon. Or you could try the old rice and boiled meat stand-by that worked for my Daphne when she had the runs. Instead of a raw meal, I gave her a couple of meals of boiled white rice and lean ground meat. Slippery elm bark coats and soothes the digestive tract, much like Pep-to Bismol (which can also be used on dogs.)

Some dogs will regurgitate their food, and then eat it again. Not an attractive sight but let him do what comes naturally, as long as it is just an occasional occurrence. Dogs will often throw up stuff they eat—mine will eat grass and vomit, almost on purpose it seems to me. Only one of my dogs vomited when he began the diet. I was alarmed at first, but once he ate it again, he was fine, with normal bowel movements later.

Problems with (ahhhem!) gas? I don't think I've smelled it around here in over two years, and Rottweilers are notorious for it! The probiotics can certainly help with this, as can yogurt high in active cultures.

Soothe That Itch

For relief of itchy skin, a quick rinse of warm water with either lemon juice or apple cider vinegar.

While some dogs experience a temporary bout of dry skin during the diet switch, symptoms lasting longer than six weeks may indicate a meat allergy. Try changing meat types and see if that makes a difference. Itching is most commonly associated with various grains, but some dogs are allergic to certain meat proteins. Also, if you are removing much of the fat, or feeding fairly lean meats, there could simply be insufficient fat in the new diet to keep his skin supple. You may notice this more in cold winter months. Kibble fed dogs often need a boost in dietary fats when it's cold and dry, too.

For relief of itchy skin, a quick rinse of warm water with either lemon juice or apple cider vinegar will soothe itchy skin. Keep your dog well brushed, but don't overdo bathing as this can worsen dandruff. Use a rinse of dilute vinegar and water to clean out the ears and to carefully wipe away tearstains from under the eyes.

Refusing to Eat

I would only worry if my dog were refusing food for more than 24 hours...

Sometimes a dog will want to skip a meal or two. That's just fine. Dogs are too smart to let themselves starve to death! When he's ready to eat again, don't feed a very large or rich meal. Listen to your dog's stomach, with your ear right up to the tummy. You should hear intermittent normal digestive gurgling and rumbling sounds. If there is a persistent absence of noise, or just occasional very high-pitched squeaks, this could indicate some sort of obstruction. Get to the vet right away. I would only worry if my dog were refusing food for more than 24 hours, especially if he also had other symptoms of illness.

A Word About Fasting

Some people fast their dogs one day a week. I don't because I don't really see the point. As far as I know, it will not hurt to fast a healthy adult dog but puppies and convalescing dogs should *not* be fasted unless on your vet's advice. And very small dogs should probably not be fasted either because of their much higher metabolisms.

Can I feed SOME raw food and kibble?

If you are going to add anything, RMBs and canned fish are your best choice.

Well, sure...some real food is better than none, as long as you feed less kibble to compensate. If you are going to add anything, RMBs and canned fish are your best choice; this way you'll be getting at least some dental benefit, and your dog will have the pleasure of chewing up really biologically appropriate food! If you feed a lot of vegetables with kibble, you run the risk of diarrhea, since kibble plus vegetables is going to be giving your dog a ton of fiber and carbohydrates. So if you feed veggies with kibble, I would use them sparingly. Honestly, I would bet that after a while of doing a "fusion" diet, you would want to stop feeding commercial food.

Am I a failure if my dog doesn't thrive on this diet?

Most of the time, dogs will have few, if any, of these problems. If your dog is lethargic, appears in pain, is vomiting or pooping blood, has a distended stomach, or appears dehydrated, take him to your vet. Some people feel more comfortable, when starting to feed raw, having a complete blood work up and fecal check done before they change diets so they have a baseline. Then they have another once the dog has settled into the new diet to monitor how the dog is faring.

One of the great things about feeding this way is the sheer number of ways you can tailor the diet for your dog.

TRUE STORY: I got Daphne from a local shelter, and the contract I had with them stipulated that she be spayed shortly after adoption. I had started her immediately on a raw diet, and she was doing very well. After the spay surgery, she became lethargic, vomiting, unwilling to eat or drink, and seemed to be in pain. I was terrified that she had some kind of bone obstruction. I took her into my vet, who agreed there was something blocking her bowel, and the poor dog was left at his office for further examination. On re-opening her up, he found that her digestive tract was completely empty of food matter—but a gauze pad had been left behind during surgery! Oops. Once that was removed, she was her bouncy, hungry self again and hasn't had a problem since.

There probably aren't many dogs that can't handle *any* raw foods. One of the great things about feeding this way is the sheer number of ways you can tailor the diet for your dog. I guess it could happen. If after a trial period of from two to four months your dog isn't thriving, or continues to have digestive problems even after you've tried adjusting the diet, or if she just flat refuses to eat, you may want to consider another type of diet. If your dog isn't thriving, you may want an experienced raw food feeder or canine nutritionist experienced with raw diets to analyze the construction of your dog's diet. They can pinpoint the areas in which your dog may be deficient. You and your dog are really partners in this venture! I've included some references in the back of the book which outline different home prepared diets. There may even be a number of alternative commercial foods that may work better for your dog if all else fails. At the very least, if you have read this book and some of the other resources I've referenced, you will have amassed a great deal of knowledge about canine nutrition and can now make a more educated choice on choosing a diet for your companion.

CHAPTER 9

The Straight Poop

No book about feeding a raw diet is really complete without a short discussion of—well, let's call it what it is—poop. Most people who feed raw start paying more attention than ever to their dog's overall condition and functioning including poop. To pick up where our dogs leave off (gotcha!) here's a quick rundown of what you might notice!

Smell, What Smell?

Your dog's poop will become practically odorless, small and usually quite firm, as long as you don't feed too many veggies at once. While on a quality kibble diet (BRF—Before Raw Foods) I had Phoebe trained where to "go" on her morning walks to a city park. I would tell her to hold it until we came within 20 feet of one of the park trash cans, and then she had permission to go. I did this

because carrying a heavy, warm, odiferous plastic bag of dog poop for three blocks really took some of the joie de vive from the morning walk. After her diet switch—oh! How nice. A little, practically odorless poop that hardly weighed anything and was really easy to pick up. Yard clean up became a breeze too. Often if the poop sits for a couple of days in the sun, it just turns to white powder and I stomp it into the ground. Try that with kibble poop. One other thing; flies don't seem interested in my dogs' poops any more.

A Field Guide to....

One day I'll make up "Complete Field Guide to Poop" complete with color photos and analyses of different droppings. Until then, here's a rundown:

If your dog has black poops all the time, check with your vet.

Little Beige Ones. These are the bone poops, often quite hard and grainy looking. You will notice virtually no odor, and they will turn white and crumbly within a couple of days exposed to the elements. It is normal for dogs to strain a bit harder to defecate on a raw diet—this helps keep the anal sacs cleaned out. If you notice your dog straining for too long, or she appears constipated, or the poops are consistently like this, you may want to increase the amount of veggies and boneless meat

Black Ones. These can look alarming. They usually occur after eating organ meats like liver, which contains a lot of iron. You may see these for several weeks after switching the diet, or if there was a build up of old stool in the colon. If your dog has black ones all the time, check with your vet. Consistent black stool, especially if it is very stinky, could indicate bleeding somewhere in the GI tract from a variety of causes.

Maroon Ones. I don't feed red beets to my dogs that often. However, they sure make pretty poo!

Orange or Green Ones. Again, these will be produced in direct correlation to the veggies fed in the previous meal. If you want to get festive and have Sparky produce red and green poops for Christmas, just make colored Veggie Glop and feed it in alternating meals. Maybe you can make candleholders or something.

Basic Brown Ones. The most common in my dogs. These also will turn white within days.

Bones! Relax. Small bone pieces are normal; I notice little pea-sized bits once in a while, usually after a turkey neck meal. Some people see larger pieces in the stool regularly and don't worry. I don't like to see that—but try this—poke the pieces (Use a stick! Not your fingers, silly goose.) Chances are, they will be quite soft and rubbery, not at all hard. Adding digestive enzymes will help him better digest the RMBs properly. Giving him meals a little higher in meat content—say a chicken back and a little ground meat on the side—will give his system time to mull over its contents too.

Mucousy Ones. I noticed these a few times with dogs just starting out. There is normal mucous in the intestinal tract, and it gets shed as a matter of course. If there's mucous for several days in a row or this becomes a frequent occurrence, take your dog and a stool sample to the vet to rule out parasites or digestive problems. Lactose intolerance can also cause this, so if he's otherwise got a clean bill of health, eliminate any dairy you may be feeding.

I don't think I paid any attention to the big smooshy poops my dogs left behind when I fed kibble. Now I watch in horrified fascination when I see cheap-kibble fed dogs ooze out these voluminous piles of smelly stuff. It is absolutely normal to get a bit obsessed about dog poop when you change to this diet. You are not alone.

CHAPTER 10

Waggin' Tale End

So there you have it. Honestly, once you get into a routine of producing and feeding, it will take very little time or effort. I cannot imagine ever buying a bag of kibble again, even high-end, human-grade kibble. I have become too used to knowing just what my dogs are eating—and they are tremendously healthy now. I enjoy making their food, and they get so much more excited about it than they ever did with doggie pellets. I feel sad that I haven't done this all along with other dogs I have owned and loved. I feel silly that I bought into the kibble myth for so long.

The old chestnut "your dog will be perfectly satisfied eating the same dog food her whole life" is a bunch of hooey, if you ask me. If that's the case, why do dogs get more excited about hot dog training treats than kibble? If kibble is so wonderful, why not use it for treats? If kibble is so satisfying, why do dogs get crazy about "people food?" Dogs will eat the same kibble for a lifetime because they have to, not because they want to. If you lived on a planet where you were denied everything tasty and had to eat human kibble to survive, that's what you would do too.

Feeding a raw diet is not a "fad diet." Raw diets and left-overs are what dogs have eaten for centuries, until someone in the food industry decided that waste products remaining after producing human food would make dandy pet food. The notion of feeding animals actual, real food instead of little pellets is simply not a fad. *Kibble* is a fad diet! And mainly, pets fed actual, unprocessed food are healthier and happier. Quite frankly, that is all the impetus I need to put in the extra hour or two a month. Isn't that what we want for our animal companions anyway? Happy pets.

Questions and Answers

QUESTION. I've heard that one shouldn't feed kibble and RMBs at the same meal.

ANSWER. Well, I've heard that too, I think it's one of those internet myths that gets bandied around. I think the rationale is that since kibble sits in the stomach for so long, harmful bacteria from raw meat has a chance to colonize and take over the world or something. Well, bones probably take longer to digest than liver, but nobody says we shouldn't feed those two items together!

I collect vintage dog care books, and from the late 19th century to the mid-seventies, the most common diet advice was to feed some sort of "dog biscuit" or bread, along with a healthy serving of raw or cooked meat. So feeding kibble and meat together is hardly a new idea!

QUESTION. What about steroids and antibiotics in commercially raised meat?

On many levels, organic is probably a much better choice.

ANSWER. Yes, they are there unless you only use organically raised meats. However, the amount of unnatural additives and chemicals your dog will be ingesting on a daily basis is still drastically less than if he were eating most brands of kibble every day. On many levels, organic is probably a much better choice. But we have to be realistic. Most people, myself included, can't afford it every day.

QUESTION. Is there a difference between ground meat and whole meat?

ANSWER. Ground meat is more likely to have harmful bacteria ground into the meat, since bacteria grow on the surface and are mixed in during processing. However, it's not really a concern for most people—dogs can handle the bacteria load well. It's usually cheaper to buy hamburger meat than a chuck roast because the fat content is a little higher. I buy ground beef, turkey, and whole ground rabbit fairly regularly. Always use common sense food hygiene with any meat – refrigerate, don't cross-contaminate with nasty things...

QUESTION. How do I get blood out of....?

ANSWER. Say you go to your local chicken dealer and pick up a case of frozen chicken backs. Then you forget about it...oopsie. So now you have blood all over the carpeting in your trunk. Well, there are products like Oxi-Clean™ and enzyme cleaners that do the job very effectively, and can be added to a load of laundry too. Hydrogen peroxide works very well, just keep applying it and blotting up until it stops fizzing on contact. Use COLD WATER because hot will set the stain for sure.

Dogs are really designed to eat meat and bones...

QUESTION. What do I say to people who think I'm weird for doing this?

ANSWER. Tell them you think they're weird for feeding little kibble thingies instead of actual food. Or tell them that dogs are really designed to eat meat and bones, and there's many people that feed this way — tell them there are a number of companies that sell raw dog food made up of real meat, bones, and vegetables!

QUESTION. What about traveling and boarding?

ANSWER. Call your area kennels and ask if they are willing—and have the refrigerator space—to feed Fido his regular diet. If they seem interested (or concerned), offer to loan them one of your raw feeding books, or point them to a good internet site, so they don't think you're an iconoclastic freak who just made up this diet. Make it really easy for a caregiver to feed by making up separate little baggies or containers for each meal.

If you're just going to be on the road for a few days, try this. Pack a cooler with ice and your RMBs in a large frozen solid chunk. The outside of the block will thaw first, and you can just peel off what you need. If you are staying at a motel, ask nearby restaurants if they will let you keep the cooler in their cold storage (REALLY I've done this!). Or use the mini-fridge in the room. Some people stop at grocery stores and buy what they need as they go.

There are also a number of commercial raw vendors who carry a line of freeze dried foods. These are concentrated and light weight, ideal for traveling.

Finally, some folks just switch back to a premium kibble, if their dog is OK with it. Whatever you do, make sure whatever you are going to feed, your dog is used to it and won't get diarrhea!

QUESTION. I'm a vegetarian – can I really do this?

You probably already give some thought to an appropriate diet for yourself and your family...

ANSWER. Certainly! You probably already give some thought to an appropriate diet for yourself and your family — this is exactly what you're going to do for your dog, and good for you! Honestly, handling the meat gets quite easy after a while. Since most of what you get will be human grade product, it will not be terribly messy. Besides, this is what meat eaters in the wild do — even many fish eat other fish. Assuming you haven't been feeding your dog a vegetarian diet up to now, consider this a much more honest and appropriate way of feeding than pouring kibble into the dish.

QUESTION. White tripe at the grocery store...?

ANSWER. No — this is bleached and processed for human consumption, and is fairly nutrition-free. There's none of the valuable enzymes or roughage, and besides which it's not smelly so your dog probably won't be as interested.

QUESTION. Is it OK ever to cook?

ANSWER. Well, I don't see why not, once in a while. Some foods like squash and carrots are more nutritious in some ways than raw. Sometimes I make omelettes for the dogs and put weird things like mackerel, bananas and zucchini in there. The garbage guts gang always eats it. A kennel website I read had the weekly menu for their dogs spelled out, and one meal was a peanut butter and wheat bread sandwich! It's up to you—you can be a real purist, and your dog will thrive. Or you can be a little relaxed sometimes —and your dog will thrive...!

QUESTION. What about weird meats like deer and cow heads?

ANSWER. I do feed deer meat, either from a local processor or neighbors who hunt. It's safe to do so in my state. I don't feed the leg bones however — my dogs crack them into scary sharp pieces; those are hard bones and make mommy nervous!

What you feed is really only limited to common sense and safety, and your own sense of adventure. I've read of people feeding snake and alligator meat. Lord knows many bugs are protein packed snacks. I've gone to a small processor for various animal parts (which incidentally get picked up for rendering into kibble). It's an ungodly messy job—not to mention my truck bed looks like a serial killer has been at work back there, and Dog forbid I get stopped by the law for a traffic infraction...! One basically has to root around in giant bins full of cow innards, raw tripe, heads, lower legs and various skeleton parts; everything swimming in a soup of blood, hair, and little bits of viscera.

I sort of enjoyed writing that!

Resources

This is by no means an exhaustive list of books, periodicals, and websites. I have only listed those I have read and relied upon for guidance both in feeding my own dogs, and in writing this book. Any of these books will have a bibliography you can refer to, should you want to read more.

Books

Dog Health & Nutrition For Dummies, M. Christine Zink, DVM, 2001
> Not really a raw feeding book, but a great book for understanding the basics of canine dietary processes, and plenty of tips on basic nutrition and health care. Dr. Zink is not a proponent of the raw food diet, but the information in her book is excellent.

Dogs, Diet, and Disease, Caroline D. Levin, 2001
> This book explores the link between commercial foods and canine illness. Not a raw-feeding book, but excellent if you have a chronically ill dog, with recipes for home made diets and tons of information for those of you caring for dogs with immune related disease.

Foods Pets Die For, Ann Martin, 2002
> The book that raised awareness about what *really* goes into many commercial pet foods. Although the author includes recipes for homemade pet meals. If you want to learn about the pet food industry, and how to decipher kibble labels, this is the book. The author is not a fan of raw feeding, though, so don't look to this book for diet info!

Give Your Dog A Bone, Ian Billinghurst, DVM, 1993

Grow Your Pups With Bones, Ian Billinghurst, DVM, 1998

The BARF Diet, Ian Billinghurst, DVM, 2001
Billinghurst popularized raw feeding with *GYDAB*, published in 1993. His latest book *The BARF Diet* is updated and practical and "how to." Thousands have relied on his books for raw feeding, however some people find that his books have so much detail that they can be overwhelming.

Natural Nutrition for Dogs and Cats: The Ultimate Diet, Kymythy R. Schultze, 1998
Schultze's book is an excellent book on raw feeding. She includes a monthly menu sheet and suggested amounts of both food and supplements for your animal companion.

The Nature of Animal Healing, Martin Goldstein DVM, 1999
Provides information on diet, disease, and alternative treatments for many illnesses and chronic conditions. Not a diet book per se — but a fascinating read, and an excellent chapter on diet and different ways of feeding.

Raw Meaty Bones, Tom Lonsdale, 2001
My personal favorite, and THE book to hand your veterinarian if he/she wants to know more about evolutionary diets. Exhaustively researched, easy and entertaining to read, promotes a very basic, simple raw diet.

Order these and many other fine dog books from MY favorite source. Dogwise, www.dogwise.com, 1-800-776-2665

Periodicals

Whole Dog Journal
WDJ covers all aspects of canine nutrition, healthcare, training, and behavior in depth every month. 1-800-829-9165
www.whole-dog-journal.com

Internet Resources

The internet has enabled many people to learn more than they thought possible about All Things Dog! Remember it is both a wealth of information as well as mis-information. Use common sense when browsing, and don't believe everything you read. Typing "raw dog diet" or "BARF" into your browser will bring up literally thousands of sites. I will leave it to you to find ones that resonate. Following are a few discussion lists that I have found particularly helpful, as well as a few supplier sites.

Discussion Groups

Dogwise.com Forums has a great group of dog forums. Authors, Dogwise staff and YOU can post questions, answers, tips and theories. I frequently participate in their "Raw Dog Food" forum. Just go to www.dogwise.com, click on FORUMS to register. Maybe we'll "meet" there!

Wellpets is a majordomo email list program—this means you have to subscribe to it via email; it cannot be read on the website. The website contains a wealth of information on natural dog care and feeding; the mailing list echoes the site content. To subscribe: http://www.listservice.net/wellpet/index.htm

Yahoo!groups Has literally hundreds of groups devoted to raw feeding (yes, including some anti-raw groups!). Search for breed-specific groups, those for specific geographical areas, for pets with special needs, service dogs, professional breeders. In the unlikely event you can't find what you're looking for, start your own group! I'm going to list just a few general groups that I have found to be very supportive. Here's their main search page: http://groups.yahoo.com/

BARF-lite: Unmoderated and very relaxed. You won't find in-depth discussions on supplements or "correct" ratios for things here, but a great place to ask general diet and health questions.

CarnivoreFeed-Supplier: Carnivore feed suppliers provides a list of what they have to offer people who feed their carnivores a natural raw diet. Pet owners list their needs. If you are looking for a particular product or referral to suppliers or groups in your area, check here.

K9Nutrition: A high volume list for people wanting to learn more about nutrition and dogs, and sharing ideas on feeding for daily use and for special needs, such as illness, recuperating, lactation, pregnancy and for all life stages. The list owner is a very knowledgeable dog and nutrition person, and many of the regulars on this list are similarly well informed and helpful.

raw-dogs.com: This is my website where you'll find more photos, more oddball questions along with answers too weird to put in the book. There are additional links to resources I have found useful.

rawfeeding: This list will give you access to an amazing amount of knowledge from people who own just one dog, to those who feed a raw diet to in excess of 30 dogs. Discussions are focused on diet only, so this is a very information-rich list for "newbies" and old hands alike.

ToyDogBARF: A list specifically for those with small or toy breeds. The list owner is a Yorkie breeder; she and the regulars here answer any question you have about feeding the little'uns.

Some Good General Raw Feeding and Nutrition Sites

There are literally thousands of websites on raw feeding—some are excellent, some are even "anti-raw," some are rather questionable, and most are pretty useful. Do not rely on any one source for all your diet advice, but if you have internet access, spend some time cruising around various websites. I'm just listing two of my favorites because they are comprehensive and well thought out.

Barfing Boxers. Another excellent site with a really useful Frequently Asked Questions page if someone is curious about the hows and whys of raw feeding, I generally refer them here. http://www.njboxers.com/faqs.htm

BowChow. Mary Straus has put together a superb website covering many aspects of dog nutrition. There's a whole page of tips and meal plans from other raw feeders, and the treats page is excellent! Tons of useful links too.
http://www.bowchow.com

Tools

Finally, places to find some of the tools you might need. Don't forget auction sites like eBay.

Maverick Grinder. Probably the most popular grinder among raw feeders — reasonably priced and even their most basic model is capable of doing most of the softer bones.
1-877-354-1265 www.pierceequipment.com

Northern Tool. Another excellent grinder. I know someone who runs a rescue for small dogs and swears by this one for grinding large amounts of meat, bones, and vegetables.
1-800-221-0516 www.northerntool.com

Vita-Mix. I adore my Vita-Mix™. It quickly reduces chunks of vegetables into glop. Not inexpensive, and you certainly don't have to have one of these for gloperizing, but it sure makes the job go fast! They also have factory reconditioned mixers—you can save a few dollars and get a guarantee.
1-800-848-2649 www.vitamix.com

Commercial Raw Food Sources

The ones that I have listed are pretty well established, but this doesn't mean that unlisted ones are inferior, just that I don't know much about them. Since raw feeding is growing in popularity, it seems there are new companies coming onto the market frequently. Some suppliers listed sell complete meals, some just meats, and many have exotic meats, both whole and ground. Not every supplier here distributes to every state. Contact them to find your closest distributor.

Bravo Raw Diet. Good pricing and variety, plus exotic meats. 1-860-693-0632 www.bravorawdiet.com

Dr. Ian Billinghurst's BARF products. BARF patties, supplements, kangaroo meat, and freeze dried patties that are excellent for boarding or traveling. www.barfworld.com

Mousies. Try these folks for yummy rodents for your small dog. www.miceonice.com

Oma's Pride. Has been around a while—complete mixes, and you add supplements if you wish. 1-800-678-6627 www.omaspride.com

Raw4Dogs. Offers both whole and ground products, and green tripe too. www.raw4dogs.com

Steve's Real Food. A complete diet, as well as cat food and freeze dried foods.1-888-526-1900 www.stevesrealfood.com

Sample Feeding Week

Just for fun, I charted the food I fed throughout a normal week. This is about as "typical" as it gets around here. A week's menu three weeks from now could have completely different meats, or simply be an "all chicken" week, depending on availability.

	A.M.	P.M.	
MON	Chicken backs	Canned salmon and green tripe	Supplements mixed with exceptionally stinky dinner.
TUE	Chicken back, ground bone-in rabbit	Chicken back and ground bone-in rabbit	
WED	Slabs of beef	Chicken back and glop	
THU	Ground turkey	Ground turkey and beef heart chunk,	Supplements with breakfast
FRI	Chicken backs	Ground rabbit, pork neck bones, glop, green tripe	
SAT	Chicken backs	Chicken backs and glop	Big beef chew bone day!
SUN	Chicken backs pork neck bones	Ground rabbit and glop	Supplements with dinner

Carina Beth MacDonald

Born 1958, Boston MA. Left US 1960. Grew up in Scotland, England, France, Turkey, several Greek islands. Hippy brat. Attended school intermittently. Graduated Portree High School, Isle of Skye, Scotland, 1975, the first girl ever to get expelled from the boarding hostel there and suspended from PHS. Tended bar intermittently from age 14 to age 21. Was an exotic dancer for a brief period of time in the U.K. Received a BA "with special commendation," Glasgow School of Art & Architecture, 1979.

Moved to California on return ticket. Got seduced by hot tubs, sunshine and cars. Stayed, started painting Victorian houses, got state painting contractors license. Lived in San Jose, Santa Cruz and Willits. 1985 lost everything in arson fire. Moved to Colorado with some guy, lived in a van and motels. Did well painting more houses, bought a house, ditched the guy. Took a break and drove a semi OTR for three years (my first Rottie came with me). Published some silly stories in trucking magazines. 1993 received a BA in psych from Metro state, still painting houses and doing arts and crafts. Spent seven years being a volunteer rape crisis counselor. Took leave of my senses (not for the first time), applied and accepted to law school, hated it and dropped out half way through. Still painting houses. Now, instead of all male biker crews I have an absolutely fabulous all female crew (not by design). Met a wonderful man in Las Vegas while visiting, moved to Michigan in 2001. Still painting and now faux painting too, get more involved in being a dog geek. Wrote book.

Have had dogs my whole life, much to my mother's dismay...I used to bring home all manner of animals, reptiles, bugs, dogs, cats, wild rodents. Fostered dogs for a while with a small rescue agency in Denver. Stole abused dogs from drug dealers a couple of times. Now am training my first dog for obedience competition and agility and have one certified therapy dog who does rest home visits. Breed of choice is Rottweilers (since 1986) but have had a number of different mutts, too.

RAW DOG FOOD

Index

sources for meats, 26-27
soy, 9
squash, 28, 29, 44, 49, 70
stabilizers, 11-12
stainless steel utensils, 15, 50
stains, removing, 69
steroids, in commercial meats, 68
stomach acids, 7
stools, 2, 52
    analysis of, 64-66
    bloody, 62, 65
    bone fragments in, 4, 65, 66
storage containers, 37
sugars, 12
supplements, nutritional, 3, 8, 10, 23, 33-35, 44

T

table scraps (leftovers), 13, 16-17, 23, 33, 67
tallow, 11
teeth
    broken, 18, 25
    cleaning, 1, 5, 17
    dental health and, 1, 8, 17-19
texturizers, 12
thyroid function, and cruciferous
    vegetables, 29
tocopherols, 12
tomatoes, 28, 29
tools, 20
tools and kitchen equipment, 36-39, 76
travel, preparing food for, 69-70
trial periods, 62-63
trichinosis, 26
tripe, types of, 28, 70
turkey
    ground, 68-69
    necks, 6, 19, 53
    wing and leg bones, 25

V

vacuum sealers, 39
vegetables, 1, 3, 6, 8, 19, 23
    calculating portion size, 45
    cooked, 70
    feeding with kibble, 61-62
    introducing, 44, 58-59
    nightshade family, 29
    organic, 42
    preparing, 28-30, 37, 48-50
    sources for, 42
    thyroid function and cruciferous
        vegetables, 29
    vegetable to meat ratio, 29
vegetarians, and raw food diets, 70
veggie glop, 6, 28-30, 42
    adding meat to, 50
    to grains ratio, 32-33
    introducing, 44
    recipe, 48-50
venison, 19, 26, 71
veterinarians
    and alternative diets, 8-9, 17-18
    digestive distress, 51, 57, 61, 62, 66
Vitamin A, 24
Vitamin C, 35, 49
Vitamin E, 12, 33, 34-35
vomiting, 60, 62

W

water, 31-32
weight control, 10, 45-46, 47, 52-55
wheat, 9, 11
white tripe, 70

Y

yeast infections, 10, 11, 17
yogurt, 3, 19, 23, 30, 44, 49, 59, 60

Also available from Dogwise Publishing

Go to www.dogwise.com for more books and ebooks.

Work Wonders
Feed Your Dog Raw Meaty Bones
Tom Lonsdale

Work Wonders leads the reader through the practical essentials of dog feeding including how to find sources, store, and prepare raw food. It also deals with risk management, junk-food induced diseases afflicting modern pets and the epidemic of canine oral disease and "dog breath." By the author of *Raw Meaty Bones*.

Unlocking the Canine Ancestral Diet
Healthier Dog Food the ABC Way
Steve Brown

Steve Brown, an expert on canine nutrition, shows how you can bring the benefits of the canine ancestral diet to your dog by feeding him differently as little as just one day a week. And no, you won't need to lead a pack of dogs on a hunting expedition! Just follow Steve's well-researched and easy to follow ABCs to make improvements to whatever your dog currently eats.

Canine Massage, 2nd Ed.
A Complete Reference Manual
Jean-Pierre Hourdebaigt, L.M.T.

Bring the well-known benefits of massage to your own dog or become a canine massage specialist. Over 100 illustrations and 100 photos, detailed examinations of muscular stress points, diagnoses, and treatments.

Canine Massage
In 3 Easy Steps DVD
Natalie Lenton

Whether you are a complete novice, or have experience with massage, this DVD is a must for every dog owner who wants to improve or maintain their dog's quality of life, mobility and comfort level. Within one hour, this DVD will give you all the knowledge you need to massage your dog like a professional.

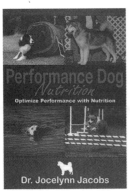

Performance Dog Nutrition
Optimize Performance with Nutrition
Dr. Jocelynn Jacobs

Get better performance from your canine athlete! Learn how to meet the special nutritional needs of your performance dog and how to meet them with a sound nutrition program. Explains how to read dog food labels and select appropriate food for your dog.

Raw Meaty Bones
Tom Lonsdale

Feeding a natural, unprocessed diet is needed now more than ever. A complete and authoritative reference on the benefits of a raw food diet for your dog. Written by Australian veterinarian Tom Lonsdale, leader in raw feeding, this exhaustively researched book provides a suggested diet, feeding tips, and do's and don'ts.

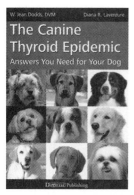

The Canine Thyroid Epidemic
Answers You Need for Your Dog
W. Jean Dodds & Diana Laverdure

If your dog is lethargic, losing his hair, gaining weight or suddenly becomes aggressive, perhaps the last thing you (or your vet!) would think about is his thyroid. Unfortunately, thyroid disorders can cause dozens of health and behavioral problems in dogs and frequently go undiagnosed or are misdiagnosed. And the real tragedy is that most thyroid problems are treatable with the right medical care and a well-informed owner.

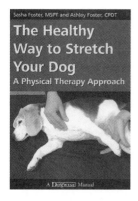

The Healthy Way to Stretch Your Dog
A Physical Therapy Approach
Sasha Foster, MSPT, CCRT and Ashley Foster, CPDT-KA

You have probably heard that humans need to stretch for good health. So do dogs. Now you can learn how to safely and effectively stretch your dog to prevent injuries, maintain joint integrity, and improve you dog's fitness whether he is an elite canine athlete or a lap dog.

The Healthy Way to Stretch Your Dog DVD
A Physical Therapy Approach with Activity Specific Stretching Routines DVD
Sasha Foster, MSPT, CCRT and Ashley Foster, CPDT-KA

This DVD demonstrates how to safely and effectively stretch each major muscle group. Teaches correct hand placement for joint stabilization and how to maintain good form. Stretching routines are presented for both large and small dogs, older dogs, and those that are involved in a variety of dog sports.

Dogwise.com your source for quality books, ebooks, DVDs, training tools and treats.

We've been selling to the dog fancier for more than 25 years and we carefully screen our products for quality information, safety, durability and FUN! You'll find something for every level of dog enthusiast on our website www.dogwise.com or drop by our store in Wenatchee, Washington.

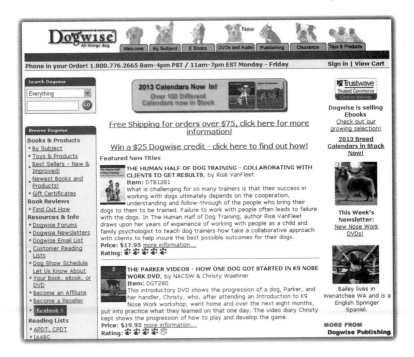